Mastering Growth Marketing

The Ultimate Guide to

Full-Funnel Growth

RISHABH DEV

Made with ❤ on the Notion Press Platform

www.notionpress.com

*"Every unicorn was once
an experiment."*

-Rishabh Dev

Contents

Acknowledgment

I would like to express my gratitude to the individuals who have generously contributed their time, knowledge, and expertise to the creation of this book, "Mastering Growth Marketing."

This book combines my experience executing growth experiments and consulting over 50 companies on growth over the past 10+ years, along with expert insights from many of my friends in the industry who are achieving great results in their respective fields.

I want to extend my deepest appreciation to all of them:

Deepak Kanakaraju, for his exceptional contribution to Email Marketing

Radhakrishnan KG, for his insights on nurture content

Raj Vasani, for his valuable input on Lead Generation and Performance Marketing

Sanjay Shenoy, for sharing his expert insights on SEO

Jayant Padhi, for his contribution to Sales Strategies

To all the individuals mentioned above, thank you for your unwavering support, dedication, and commitment to excellence in your respective fields.

Your contributions have undoubtedly significantly impacted the quality and depth of this book.

I would also like to thank Shreyak Karmacharya who has helped me edit the book and contributed the graphics to bring my concepts to visual life.

Finally, I would like to thank all my readers for their continued support and trust. It is my sincerest hope that "Mastering Growth Marketing" will serve as a valuable resource and guide as you navigate the world of growth marketing.

Thank you all for being a part of this incredible journey.

Rishabh Dev

Introduction

Welcome to "Mastering Growth Marketing," a book that will equip you with the knowledge and skills needed to thrive in the dynamic world of growth marketing. Whether you are a seasoned marketer seeking to sharpen your expertise or a budding professional looking to embark on a successful growth marketing journey, this book is tailored to meet your needs.

In this fast-paced era of digital transformation, growth marketing has emerged as a strategic approach to drive sustainable business growth. It goes beyond traditional marketing practices and embraces a mindset that constantly seeks innovation, adaptation, and optimization. By adopting a data-driven, customer-centric approach, growth marketers are able to identify and capitalize on untapped opportunities, leverage emerging technologies, and maximize results.

Part 1, "Fundamentals," lays the groundwork by demystifying growth marketing, exploring its key concepts, and helping you develop the growth mindset necessary for success. We delve into the essential skills required to drive growth, and guide you through the growth marketing process, from research to generating growth ideas and executing experiments.

Part 2, "Generalist," takes a deep dive into the growth funnel and its four key stages: awareness, customer acquisition, activation, and user retention. Through practical insights and actionable strategies, you will learn how to hack each stage of the funnel, optimize conversions, and drive revenue growth. Think lean, agile, and data-driven, as we explore the power of analytics to track and measure your growth initiatives.

Part 3, "Specialist," features guest chapters from industry experts who specialize in specific areas of growth marketing. From copywriting and content hacks to email marketing, social media, lead generation funnels, performance marketing campaigns, SEO hacking, and sales strategies, these chapters provide a wealth of knowledge and best practices to level up your growth marketing game.

Part 4, "Evolution," focuses on scaling your growth efforts and creating workflows that enable sustainable growth. We explore the power of other people's networks (OPNs) and other people's audiences (OPAs) to amplify your growth, and guide you in finding your winning growth stack. Finally, we delve into the vital aspect of measuring success as a growth marketer and understanding the key metrics that matter.

Throughout this book, we combine real-world case studies, practical examples, and hands-on exercises to ensure that you have a well-rounded understanding of growth marketing principles and their application. Whether you are an entrepreneur, marketer, or business professional, "Mastering Growth Marketing" will unlock the strategies and tactics needed to propel your business forward.

We hope this book serves as your go-to resource for mastering growth marketing and achieving sustainable business growth. Get ready to embark on an exciting journey where innovation, optimization, and customer-centricity are your guiding principles. Let us dive in and revolutionize the way you approach growth.

Happy growing!

PART 1: FUNDAMENTALS

Chapter 1

What is Growth Marketing?

Welcome to the growth marketing book. In this chapter, we will define growth marketing and explore its key concepts and principles.

Defining Growth Marketing

Growth marketing is a strategic approach to marketing that focuses on achieving specific goals or metrics through lean and agile experimentation. It involves testing and finding impactful and scalable ways to reach a specific goal or focus metric, known as the north star.

One of the key principles of growth marketing is achieving desired outcomes with the least possible resources, including manpower, time, and money. This is achieved through a lean and agile approach that emphasizes continuous experimentation and optimization.

Lean & Agile

In a world where resources are limited, it is essential to make the most of what we have. Lean principles help us to do just that.

The term "lean" refers to the practice of achieving desired outcomes with fewer resources, emphasizing efficiency, and minimizing waste. By adopting lean principles, growth marketers can focus on identifying the most effective strategies and tactics to drive growth while optimizing resource allocation.

On the other hand, the term "agile" pertains to the ability to adapt and respond quickly to changes and feedback. Growth marketers employ agile methodologies to rapidly test and iterate on their marketing campaigns and initiatives, enabling them to gather data and insights in real time.

This iterative approach allows growth marketers to refine their strategies continuously, capitalize on successful tactics, and course-correct when necessary, ensuring optimal outcomes and continuous improvement.

In the context of growth marketing, by adopting these principles, growth marketers can optimize their resources, test, and iterate on their strategies, and achieve their north star goals with greater efficiency and effectiveness.

Growth Marketing as an Overlap of Product and Marketing

Growth marketing draws from both product and marketing disciplines. It recognizes that the product itself plays a vital role in driving growth. By understanding the product and leveraging marketing strategies, we can create a holistic approach to achieving our goals.

In the traditional marketing approach, the product is seen as a separate entity from the marketing efforts. However, growth marketing recognizes that the product and marketing are inherently intertwined. The product itself is a key driver of growth and can be leveraged to achieve marketing goals.

Growth marketing methods often rely on the product itself. By understanding the product's unique value proposition and features, growth marketers can create targeted marketing campaigns that resonate with their target audience. This approach allows growth marketers to create a seamless experience for the user, from the first point of contact with the product to the final purchase decision.

In addition to leveraging the product itself, growth marketing also relies on traditional marketing strategies such as SEO, social media, and content marketing. By combining these strategies with a deep understanding of the product, growth marketers can create a holistic approach to achieving their goals.

The North Star Metric

A critical component of growth marketing is the identification of a north star metric, which serves as the primary focus or goal that guides the entire business. This metric encapsulates the core value or desired outcome that the business aims to deliver to its customers.

By aligning efforts towards the north star metric, growth marketers can effectively drive growth and measure success. This approach allows businesses to focus their resources and efforts on achieving a specific outcome, rather than spreading themselves too thin and diluting their impact.

As a growth leader, it is critical to translate something that looks ambiguous or undefined into something specific and measurable within a given timeline. This requires a deep understanding of the business and its goals, as well as the ability to identify key metrics that align with those goals.

Growth marketing was initially built for startups, but its lean and agile methodologies can be equally viable for bigger businesses looking to achieve the same results with fewer resources.

Even the largest corporations in the world have adopted growth marketing processes to get those results without using the same number of resources as before.

Therefore, growth marketing can be valuable for businesses of any size. In this course, learners will build the necessary mindset, skill set, process, and toolset to achieve their growth marketing goals.

By understanding the principles of growth marketing and learning how to apply them in practice, learners will be able to drive growth and achieve their north star metric, regardless of the size of their business.

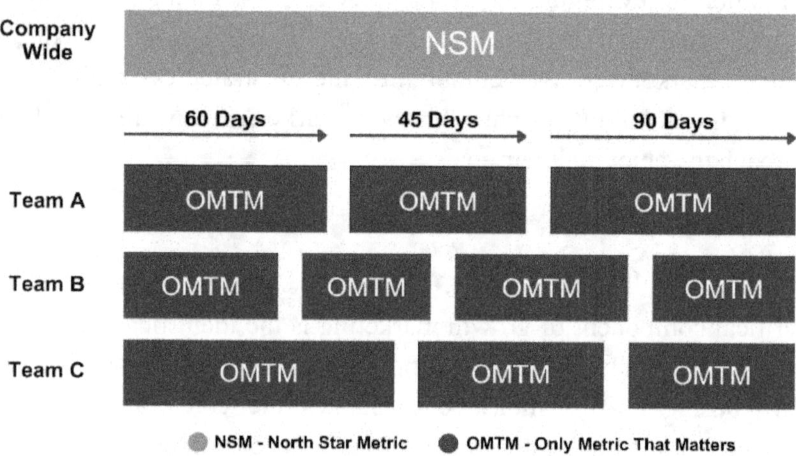

Growth Marketing as The Superset of Marketing Experiments

Growth marketing encompasses a wide range of channels, methods, and tools that fall into other areas of marketing.

These channels, methods, and tools often fall into other areas of marketing:

- Paid methods of awareness of acquisition (Digital Marketing)
- Organic methods of awareness and acquisition (Digital Marketing)
- Unconventional methods and offbeat channels (Creative Marketing)
- Other People's Networks (Growth Hacking)
- Influencers, Affiliates, Referrals
- Other People's APIs

- Other People's Communities (and so on)
- Viral Mechanics (Technical Marketing)
- Marketing Automation (Technical Marketing)
- Behavioural Psychology (Growth Hacking)
- Lean Analytics (Data-Driven Marketing)
- …ENDLESS POSSIBILITIES.

As a result, growth marketing can be seen as a superset of other marketing approaches and channels like digital marketing, growth hacking, technical marketing, and creative marketing. By combining these approaches and leveraging a variety of channels and tools, growth marketers can create targeted campaigns that drive growth and achieve their north star metric.

The possibilities with growth marketing are endless. By adopting a growth mindset and embracing a culture of experimentation and iteration, growth marketers can continuously refine and optimize their strategies, leveraging new channels and tools as they emerge.

Growth Marketing as a Full-Funnel Approach to Marketing

While digital marketing covers the stages of the funnel including awareness and acquisition, growth marketing is a full-funnel marketing approach covering all the stages of an ideal customer's journey – which are the stages of Awareness, Acquisition, Activation, Revenue, Retention, and Referral.

By considering the entire funnel, growth marketers ensure a comprehensive and cohesive approach to drive growth across the entire customer lifecycle. This approach allows businesses to not only acquire new customers but also retain and grow their existing customer base.

This is the key difference between digital marketing and growth marketing, and why growth marketing can also be seen as full-funnel marketing. While digital marketing focuses on specific stages of the funnel, growth marketing takes a holistic approach to the entire customer journey.

In the next chapter, we will dive deeper into each stage of the funnel and explore how growth marketers can leverage different channels, methods, and tools to drive growth at each stage.

Chapter 2

Growth Marketing vs Digital Marketing

One might wonder what the difference is between digital marketing and growth marketing. The answer to this question is best explained with a simple analogy: the horse vs unicorn analogy.

The Horse vs Unicorn Analogy

Imagine you are a horse, staying in the barn or the shed. Once outside, you run straight to the destination taking the same path as all the other horses.

This is equivalent to targeting the most common and saturated channels that all other marketers are focusing on. You run the campaigns long enough only to realize the results are not as expected rather late.

As a horse, you will also be, to some extent, thinking within the boundaries of these digital channels. You will be limited by your own mindset and approach, and you may not be willing to experiment or try new things.

Now, imagine you are a unicorn. You are wild, you experiment, you execute faster, and you try out new channels and paths each time.

Some may think the unicorn is crazy and lives in a fantasy world. But That is where the unicorn will find amazing results faster and better in lesser budgets and lesser time than the horse.

The unicorn is not limited by the same mindset and approach as the horse. Instead, the unicorn is willing to take risks, try new things, and think outside the box. This is where growth marketing comes in.

Growth marketing is about experimenting, testing, and iterating quickly to find the best channels and strategies for growth.

It is about being willing to take risks and try new things, even if they seem crazy or unconventional. Growth marketers are like unicorns, willing to explore new territory and find new ways to reach their target audience.

Digital marketing, on the other hand, is more focused on the traditional channels and strategies that have been proven to work in the past. Digital marketers are like horses, running the same path as all the other horses, and not willing to venture outside of their comfort zone.

In order to be successful in today's fast-paced digital landscape, it is important to be both a horse and a unicorn.

You need to have the foundation of digital marketing knowledge and expertise, but you also need to be willing to experiment and try new things in order to achieve growth.

So, the next time someone asks you the difference between digital marketing and growth marketing, remember the horse vs unicorn analogy.

Think about whether you want to be a horse, limited by your mindset and approach, or a unicorn, willing to explore new territory and find new ways to reach your target audience.

Process Comparison

Here is an overview of the digital marketing process:

- Identify the goals of the brand
- Create user personas
- Create a campaign strategy
- Execute on popular channels
- Analyse campaign metrics

Now, compare this to the Growth Marketing process:

- Identify one single goal to focus on at a time (called the north star metric)
- Create user personas
- Create channel personas (what kinds of platforms do the users hang out on? or what other apps do the users install? What are

the Other People's Networks we can leverage to find my user personas?)

- Use data and gut feeling to brainstorm creative growth experiments

- Execute on selected, often offbeat channels, and analyse the north star metric

- Integrate the successful experiments into their process

So given the level of experimentation, the scope of trying new channels based on channel personas, and going outside of the popular track makes a unicorn what it is – MAGICAL!

Another angle to consider while understanding the difference between growth marketing and digital marketing is the marketing funnel.

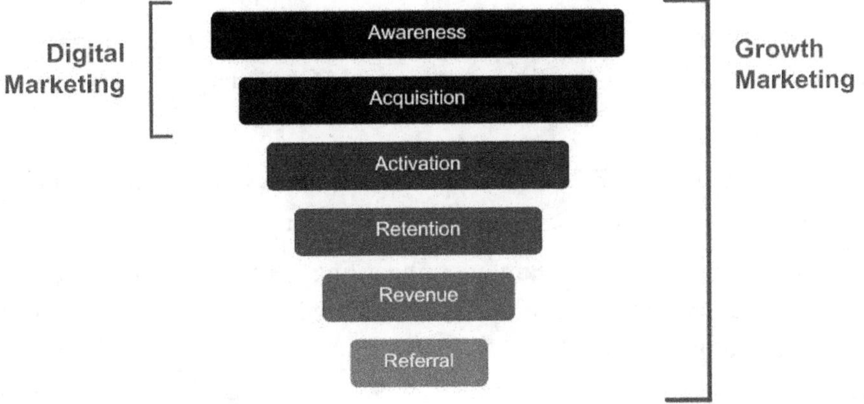

Growth Marketing is Full Funnel Marketing

Growth marketing covers the entire funnel, from awareness to referral, while digital marketing primarily focuses on awareness and acquisition through channels like ads, social media, and SEO.

This is known as the A3R3 funnel, which stands for Awareness, Acquisition, Activation, Revenue, Retention, and Referral2.

To illustrate each stage of the A3R3 funnel, we will explore some examples from different startups.

Awareness

One of the best examples of a company that has successfully leveraged growth marketing to generate awareness is Airbnb. By focusing on user-generated content and social media campaigns, Airbnb was able to reach a broader audience and establish its brand presence.

The company encouraged users to share their experiences on social media, which generated a significant amount of user-generated content and helped to attract more customers.

Acquisition

Dropbox is a classic example of a company that used growth hacking to achieve rapid user acquisition. The company offered additional free storage to users who referred their friends, driving user acquisition through word-of-mouth and viral loops.

In a Forbes article, it was reported that this strategy helped Dropbox to grow from 100,000 to 4 million users in just 15 months.

Activation

Slack is a great example of a company that has successfully implemented growth marketing strategies to increase activation rates.

The company provided a seamless onboarding experience for new users, which increased activation rates and encouraged users to become active and engaged in their platform.

Revenue

Spotify is a great example of a company that has successfully implemented growth marketing strategies to drive revenue growth.

The company implemented personalized recommendations and targeted ads based on user preferences, which encouraged users to upgrade to premium subscriptions and purchase additional products or services.

Retention

Netflix is a great example of a company that has successfully implemented growth marketing strategies to improve user retention.

The company utilized data-driven personalization and content recommendations to keep users engaged and reduce churn rates.

Referral

Uber is a great example of a company that has successfully implemented growth marketing strategies to drive customer acquisition through word-of-mouth marketing.

The company leveraged a referral program that rewarded both new users and existing customers for referring others, leading to rapid growth and customer acquisition.

By optimizing each stage of the A3R3 funnel, businesses can achieve sustainable and scalable growth.

Here is an overview of the stages of the funnel, with examples of growth marketing strategies for each stage:

Stage	Examples
Awareness	Online Advertising, Social Media Campaigns, Influencer Partnerships
Acquisition	Referral Codes, Promotional Discounts, First-ride Coupons
Activation	Streamlined Onboarding Process, Quick Account Creation
Revenue	Transparent Pricing, Surge Pricing During Peak Times
Retention	Personalized Promotions, Loyalty Programs, Excellent Customer Support
Referral	Referral Incentives, Unique Referral Codes, Word-of-Mouth Marketing

In conclusion, digital marketing tends to focus on specific stages of the funnel, such as lead generation or conversion.

While effective, these strategies may not be sufficient for driving long-term growth.

To succeed in growth marketing, businesses must adopt a mindset that embraces experimentation, unconventional channels, and data-driven decision-making. This requires a willingness to take risks and try new approaches, as well as a deep understanding of customer behaviour and preferences.

By developing a growth mindset, businesses can differentiate themselves from competitors and unlock the full potential of their marketing efforts.

In the next chapter, we will explore practical tips and strategies for cultivating a growth mindset and achieving sustainable growth through marketing.

Chapter 3

The Mindset for Growth

Have you ever wondered what sets successful growth marketers apart from the rest? It is not just about having a set of skills or tools, but also a unique mindset that drives their approach.

Take for example, a growth team that is constantly experimenting and making data-driven decisions. They are not afraid to challenge conventional marketing methods and think creatively to find alternative solutions.

In fact, they stay thin and agile, reducing waste and optimizing their efforts for maximum impact.

The growth marketing mindset challenges conventional methods and welcomes new strategies to achieve growth.

Throughout this chapter, we will explore the various elements that make up the growth marketing mindset and examine how they play a vital role in driving the success of growth marketing.

I call these "brain tattoos" - not the permanent kind, of course, but the kind that sticks with you and shapes the way you think about marketing.

Think of it like a cool tattoo that you got on a wild night out, but instead of being on your skin, it is etched into your brain. And just like a tattoo, the growth marketing mindset is something that you will carry with you for a long time, helping you to approach marketing challenges with creativity, agility, and a healthy dose of scepticism towards conventional methods.

How to Develop the Growth Marketing Mindset Using 5 Brain Tattoos

To develop the growth marketing mindset, there are five key principles, or "brain tattoos", that one must incorporate.

1. Always Doubt the Default

Doubting the default is a critical step in thinking beyond common and saturated marketing channels and methods. It enables marketers to explore new ideas, channels, and growth hacks that go beyond the norm.

By questioning the default approach, marketers can find alternative paths to their goals and achieve growth more effectively.

Growth marketers should actively seek out diverse perspectives and opinions, including those that challenge prevailing beliefs or norms.

This can involve engaging with colleagues, industry experts, or even conducting customer research to understand different viewpoints.

Listening to diverse opinions, including those that may differ from one's own, can lead to uncovering new insights, identifying blind spots, and considering alternative approaches.

For example, Nike challenged the default approach of traditional advertising by creating a digital community for runners called Nike+. This allowed them to connect with their audience on a more personal level and offer personalized training programs and gear recommendations.

This approach helped Nike to achieve significant growth and establish a strong brand identity in the fitness industry.

2. Always be Experimenting

Experimentation is a crucial aspect of growth marketing. By constantly trying out new ideas and strategies, marketers can learn from both their successes and failures

This helps them gain valuable insights and refine their approach to achieve better results.

A mindset of continuous experimentation enables marketers to stay ahead of the competition and discover innovative approaches.

For instance, Airbnb is a famous brand that has successfully adopted a culture of experimentation. They constantly test different features and user experiences on their platform to improve the overall customer experience.

Through experimentation, they have been able to identify and launch new offerings such as Airbnb Experiences, which has helped them to expand their business and increase revenue.

3. Focus on Your North Star

To avoid getting overwhelmed and maintain focus, it is crucial for growth marketers to identify the one metric that matters the most, also known as the north star metric

By narrowing their focus to a specific goal, marketers can prioritize their efforts and ensure that their campaigns and experiments align with the most critical objectives.

For instance, Facebook's north star metric is Daily Active Users (DAUs). Everything the company does is geared towards increasing the number of DAUs as it is the key metric that drives their business growth.

Over the years, Facebook has been able to develop new features and functionalities that keep users engaged on the platform, leading to increased revenue and market share by focusing on this one metric.

4. Think Lean and Agile

The lean and agile mindsets are crucial for growth marketing. The lean mindset focuses on eliminating waste and optimizing the marketing system, while the agile mindset emphasizes delivering value quickly through shorter cycles of experimentation.

By incorporating both mindsets, marketers can streamline their processes, reduce costs, and respond effectively to market changes.

For example, Amazon is a famous brand that has successfully incorporated both the lean and agile mindsets. The company's lean approach involves eliminating unnecessary steps in their supply chain and optimizing their logistics system to reduce costs and improve efficiency.

On the other hand, their agile approach involves quickly testing and launching new products and features, such as Amazon Prime, to meet the changing needs of their customers. By combining both mindsets, Amazon has been able to maintain its position as a leading e-commerce giant and continue to grow its business.

5. Trust the Process & Think Like a Scientist

Achieving sustainable and repeatable growth requires a well-defined growth marketing process rather than relying on individual hacks or tactics.

Trusting the process involves gathering data, targeting key metrics, generating ideas, conducting experiments, implementing tools and resources, and adapting strategies based on campaign evolution.

Embracing the process is essential for achieving long-term growth.

Uber is a famous brand that has successfully adopted a growth marketing process. They started by targeting a specific niche audience, early adopters in metropolitan areas, and then used data-driven experimentation to validate their marketing strategies and drive growth.

They implemented referral marketing, which incentivized existing users to invite their friends to use the platform, resulting in significant growth.

They also experimented with different pricing strategies and promotions to attract new users and retain existing ones.

By following a systematic approach to growth marketing, Uber was able to achieve sustainable and repeatable growth and become the leading ride-sharing company worldwide.

The growth marketing process can be likened to the scientific method of testing.

Just as scientists follow a systematic approach to validate hypotheses and discover new knowledge, growth marketers use a similar process to validate marketing strategies and drive business growth.

Here is an overview of how the growth marketing process aligns with the scientific method:

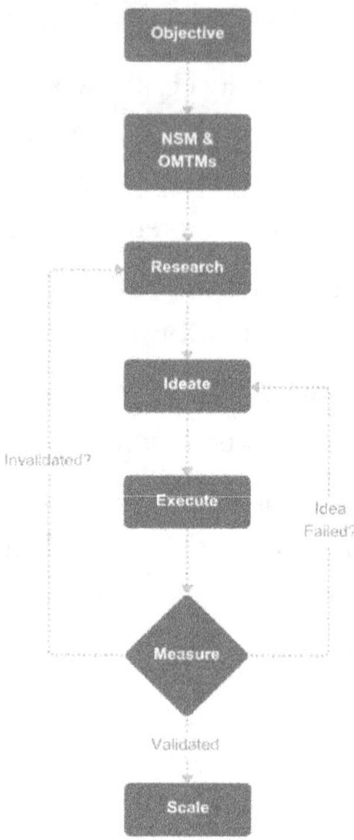

Define the Objective

In the scientific method, researchers start by defining a clear objective or research question. Similarly, growth marketers begin by identifying the desired outcome or growth goal they want to achieve. This could be increasing user engagement, acquiring more customers, or improving conversion rates.

Generate Hypotheses

Scientists form hypotheses to explain phenomena or predict outcomes. Likewise, growth marketers generate hypotheses about marketing strategies or tactics that could potentially drive growth.

Design Experiments

In the scientific method, experiments are designed to test hypotheses and collect data. Similarly, growth marketers design experiments to test their marketing hypotheses.

Execute Experiments

Scientists carry out experiments under controlled conditions to gather data and observe outcomes. Growth marketers execute their planned marketing experiments, such as A/B tests, landing page variations, or different ad campaigns, while tracking key performance indicators (KPIs) and metrics.

Analyse Data

In the scientific method, data collected from experiments is analysed to draw conclusions and evaluate the hypotheses. Growth marketers analyse the data collected during their experiments to assess the performance and effectiveness of their marketing strategies. They look for patterns, insights, and correlations to determine the impact on growth metrics.

Draw Insights

Based on the analysis of data, scientists draw insights and make conclusions about the validity of their hypotheses. Similarly, growth marketers draw insights from data analysis to understand which marketing strategies are effective and contribute to growth.

Iterate and Optimize

In the scientific method, researchers iterate and refine their hypotheses, experiments, and methodologies based on the insights gained. Growth marketers follow a similar iterative process, refining their marketing strategies, campaigns, and tactics based on the insights gained from data analysis.

Scale and Implement

Once a hypothesis has been validated and proven successful, scientists seek to scale their findings and apply them to real-world applications. Similarly, growth marketers scale their successful marketing strategies and implement them on a broader scale to drive sustainable growth for the business.

By aligning the growth marketing process with the scientific method, growth marketers can approach marketing challenges with a systematic and data-driven approach. This enables them to test and validate hypotheses, optimize their strategies, and achieve sustainable growth for their business.

With this analogy, let us dip deeper into the growth marketing process in the next chapter.

Chapter 4

Growth Marketing Skills

As you grow in your career and move to growth management or growth leadership, your core and generalist skill sets will become more important, as you will have teams taking care of the specializations. Growth Marketing requires multiple skills.

All growth marketing skills can be categorized into 3 different buckets.

1. Core Growth Skills

2. Generalist Growth Skills

3. Specialist Growth Skills

The core skills are the must-have skills and include the growth mindset, research, idea generation, and lean analytics.

Generalist skills, on the other hand, are the skills required to become a generalist growth marketer and include A/B testing, copywriting, conversion rate optimization, understanding user behaviour, setting North Star metrics, and leveraging networks.

Lastly, specialist skills are necessary for becoming a specialist in a particular area of growth marketing, such as email marketing or influencer marketing.

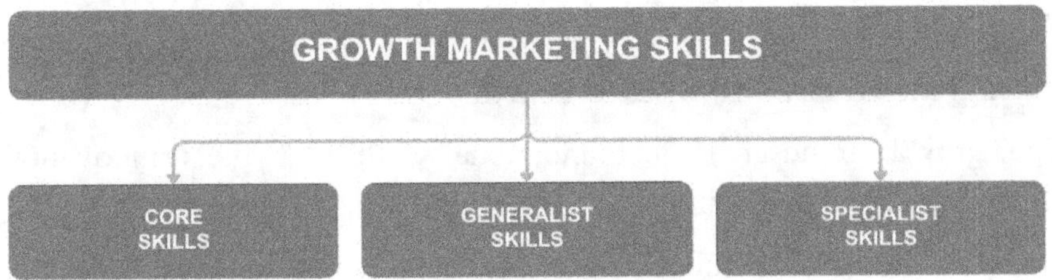

Core Growth Skills

The core or fundamental growth skills are a must-learn for all growth hackers and growth marketers.

These skills form the basis for developing effective growth strategies and executing successful campaigns.

You will be able to apply these skills to each step of the process and soon they will become second nature to you as a growth marketer.

Here are some of the abilities that will build up your core. You can spend dedicated time on these skills and polish them with repeated execution.

Managing the Growth Marketing Process

This core growth skill involves the ability to effectively manage and oversee the entire growth marketing process. It includes setting goals and objectives, developing strategies, executing campaigns, and analysing results.

A growth marketer with strong project management skills can ensure that initiatives are implemented smoothly, deadlines are met, and resources are utilized efficiently.

Being Able to Visualize the Growth Funnel

Visualizing the growth funnel is essential for understanding the user journey and identifying opportunities for improvement at each stage.

A growth marketer who can map out the funnel visually can identify potential bottlenecks, optimize conversion rates, and design targeted campaigns to move users through the funnel effectively.

This skill allows for a comprehensive view of the customer acquisition process and aids in strategic decision-making.

Putting the Growth Mindset to Practice

The growth mindset is a foundational skill that fuels innovation, experimentation, and continuous learning.

Applying the growth mindset involves embracing challenges, viewing failures as learning opportunities, and persistently seeking new solutions.

A growth marketer with a growth mindset is open to testing new ideas, adapting strategies based on data, and continuously improving performance.

Data-Based Decision Making

Data-based decision making is crucial in growth marketing. It involves collecting, analysing, and interpreting data to drive insights and make informed decisions.

A growth marketer who can effectively utilize data from various sources, such as analytics platforms, user behaviour tracking tools, and customer feedback, can identify trends, uncover user preferences, and optimize campaigns for maximum impact.

Understanding and Mapping the User's Journey

Understanding the user's journey is essential for designing personalized experiences and delivering the right message at the right time.

A growth marketer who can empathize with users, identify touchpoints, and map out their journey from awareness to conversion can tailor marketing strategies to align with user needs and expectations.

This skill enables marketers to optimize the user experience, increase engagement, and drive conversions.

Ability to Understand and Leverage OPNs and Piggybacking

OPNs (Other People's Networks) and piggybacking refer to leveraging existing networks, partnerships, or platforms to expand reach and acquire new customers.

A growth marketer who understands how to identify and tap into relevant OPNs can accelerate growth by gaining access to pre-existing audiences.

This skill involves strategic collaborations, influencer partnerships, and joint marketing efforts that amplify brand exposure and attract new customers.

Identifying and Ideating on Growth Channels

Identifying effective growth channels involves staying updated on industry trends, exploring new marketing platforms, and understanding where the target audience is most active.

A growth marketer skilled in channel identification can assess the potential of various channels (e.g., social media, content marketing, paid advertising) and determine which ones align best with the business's goals and target market.

This skill allows for strategic allocation of resources and optimal channel selection for maximum growth impact.

By cultivating and expanding on these core growth skills, growth marketers can enhance their ability to drive growth and deliver impactful results. Each skill contributes to a well-rounded and data-driven approach, enabling marketers to navigate the complex landscape of growth marketing and stay ahead of the competition.

Remember, as you grow into management roles, you will mostly be executing your core skills along with managing the team. These skills will help you make high-level decisions.

Generalist Growth Skills

The general skillset is a set of growth marketing skills marketers develop with execution. These skills apply across different types of growth experimentation.

To become a generalist growth hacker or growth marketer, these skills are required:

Psychology for Growth

Psychology plays a crucial role in understanding consumer behaviour, motivations, and decision-making processes. A growth marketer who possesses a strong understanding of psychology can leverage this knowledge to create persuasive messaging, optimize user experiences, and drive conversions.

By applying psychological principles such as social proof, scarcity, and cognitive biases, marketers can influence user behaviour and enhance the effectiveness of their growth strategies.

Copy & Content for Growth

Content is a powerful tool for attracting, engaging, and retaining customers. A growth marketer skilled in content creation and strategy can develop compelling and valuable content that resonates with the target audience.

This includes creating blog posts, articles, videos, infographics, and other formats that align with the audience's preferences and address their pain points.

Effective content marketing drives organic traffic, establishes thought leadership, and cultivates brand loyalty.

Design for Growth

Design plays a crucial role in shaping the user experience and influencing user behaviour. A growth marketer who understands design principles can create visually appealing and intuitive interfaces that enhance engagement and conversions.

This skill involves knowledge of user interface (UI) and user experience (UX) design, information architecture, visual hierarchy, and responsive design.

By optimizing the design elements of websites, landing pages, and marketing collateral, growth marketers can improve the overall user experience and drive growth.

Technology for Growth

Technology is a key enabler of growth marketing initiatives. A growth marketer who is adept at leveraging marketing technologies, tools, and platforms can streamline processes, automate tasks, and gather valuable insights.

This skill involves familiarity with customer relationship management (CRM) systems, marketing automation tools, email marketing platforms, analytics software, and other relevant technologies.

By effectively utilizing technology, growth marketers can enhance efficiency, personalize experiences, and scale marketing efforts.

Analytics for Growth

Analytics is the foundation of data-driven growth marketing. A growth marketer skilled in analytics can collect, interpret, and derive actionable insights from data to optimize campaigns and drive growth.

This skill includes proficiency in web analytics tools (e.g., Google Analytics), data visualization techniques, and statistical analysis. By tracking key performance indicators (KPIs), monitoring user behaviour, and conducting data-driven experiments, growth marketers can make informed decisions and continually refine their strategies.

CRO & A/B Testing for Growth

Conversion rate optimization (CRO) and A/B testing are essential skills for optimizing the user journey and improving conversion rates. A growth marketer who understands CRO principles can identify areas of improvement, develop hypotheses, and conduct A/B tests to validate assumptions and implement data-driven optimizations.

This skill involves designing and implementing experiments, analysing results, and iterating based on insights gained. By continuously refining conversion funnels and user experiences, growth marketers can maximize conversions and drive sustainable growth.

These generalist growth skills are critical for growth marketers to have a broad understanding and proficiency in various areas of growth marketing.

Most growth marketing managers will be good at all of these areas, and may have past experience in a few specific channels, which we will discuss next.

Specialist Growth Skills

You are not required to learn all these skills.

Building expertise in 1 or more of these skills will make you a well-rounded T-shaped marketer:

- Email Marketing
- Influencer Marketing
- Performance Marketing
- Paid search
- Competitor Analytics
- Organic search

- Lead Generation
- Sales Copywriting
- Affiliate Marketing
- Referral Marketing
- Viral Mechanics
- App Marketing
- Blogging
- Sales Funnels
- Marketing Automation
- Landing page Optimization
- Ecommerce Marketing
- Front-end Development
- Web Scraping
- Mobile Marketing
- Video Marketing
- Data Visualization
- Sales Outreach
- Branding & Storytelling
- Graphics Design
- Google Analytics
- Ecommerce Analytics
- SaaS Analytics
- UI/UX
- AI
- …This list is endless!

We will not go into each skill as it is an endless list!

However, for the specific skill set, I recommend you execute various kinds of growth experiments in different industries.

This will help you learn different tools and observe different processes to grow your specific skills.

Finally, it is important to pick the right specialized skills for you.

There are various options for skills, ranging from mobile app growth to referral campaigns, influencer campaigns, affiliate marketing, lead generation, and more.

The order in which one chooses to develop core, generalist, and specialist skills does not matter.

Someone who starts with a deep specialization can always add generalist skills to improve their specialization.

However, if you are starting from scratch, you have an advantage in that you can build the mindset and learn the process first so you can see the 10,000 feet view and then go deep into your specialization.

The ultimate goal is to deploy the growth marketing process mindset and process into the selected specialization.

Chapter 5

The Growth Marketing Process

The growth marketing process can be defined in 4 phases:

- PHASE 1: The Research Phase (Find opportunities)
- PHASE 2: The Ideate Phase (Innovate ideas)
- PHASE 3: The Experiment Phase (Run experiments)
- PHASE 4: The Scale Phase (Expand what works)

The F.I.R.E framework

You can remember the process easily using the 'FIRE framework.'

- F - Find opportunities
- I - Innovate ideas
- R - Run experiments
- E - Expand what works

This FIRE framework is the key to any successful marketing or growth process. It also applied to many other areas of life and work.

Process Overview

The first phase includes researching the business and competitors. (Phase 1)

The research naturally leads to ideas (Phase 2), post which we run experiments and measure results. (Phase 3)

If the experiment is successful, it can be scaled, and if it fails, the experiment is invalidated, and the process starts again. (Phase 4)

Phase 1: RESEARCH

In the Research Phase, we need to go through the following steps:

- Deep dive into the **existing data** to find valuable data points
- **Questionnaires** with the startup founders and teams to dig for both qualitative and quantitative data
- Collecting all the data along with observations in a **growth marketing research document**

The Research Phase usually starts with a questionnaire to be filled out by the founder or business owner or key decision-maker.

Questions vary from business to business and are designed based on the first interaction with the business.

They may be different for each business based on their requirements and where they are currently at in their startup or business phase.

Here are 10 questions that I have found to be most useful while conducting business research:

- What is your north star metric? (6-month goal)
- What is your OMTM? (30-day goal)
- What is your current strategy to reach your goals?
- Describe your ideal target persona
- What is your top value proposition?
- What channels are you currently using to reach your audience?
- What offer are you currently offering and how is it doing in terms of conversions?
- Who are your top 3 competitors?
- What are the communities or other channels your target audience is active on?
- What past data do you have from your past campaigns?

With time, experience, and lots and lots of DATA, your **gut feeling** guides you to ask the right questions which then leads you to the right growth ideas and experiments.

Phase 2: IDEATE

The steps in this ideation phase include:

- Using the data from Phase 1 to list growth marketing ideas
- Fetching ideas with **past data** available from my database of growth marketing ideas
- **Brainstorming** the ideas internally and externally
- Assigning **supporting data points** to each idea
- **Mapping** each idea to the target growth metric

*Note that if you are an experienced growth marketer, it is very important to maintain a database of growth marketing ideas and to assign a score to them based on how they worked for you in the past.

Of course, the implementation will be different for new businesses or startups you work with but this will give you an idea over time how your ideas performed.

Next, the supporting data points must be assigned to each idea as shown in my template below:

Ideas These will be polished and shortlisted as growth experiments	Supporting Data or Reference The data that supports the idea or the references wherein we are leveraging other people's data	Next Steps These will convert to shortlisted experiments
Drip campaigns via messenger		
Quora top writers feature		
Side-project marketing		
Vanity dashboards are referral channels		
YouTube influencer channel partnerships		

Podcast outreach campaigns		

As you can see in the ideation template, we have the following columns in this phase:

1. **IDEAS**

2. **SUPPORTING DATA OR REFERENCE**

3. **NEXT STEPS**

The output of this phase is coming up with the first set of growth experiment ideas.

You can start with as many ideas as you like – I usually like to work with 10 ideas in the first cycle of Ideation.

The ideas are documented based on past data, channel personas, and marketing ideas.

Channel personas are characteristics of the potential new channels we can explore for growth marketing campaigns as we start thinking outside of the most popular channels.

Growth marketing is effective when we execute creative experiments on popular channels and it is also effective when we execute regular experiments on offbeat channels.

The reasons for going **beyond the popular channels** are as follows:

- The most popular channels are expensive and saturated

- There are higher chances for successful growth hacking experiments in channels that are in the early-adopters stage

- A channel's effectiveness typically reduces over time

- Offbeat and new channels are mostly cheaper than saturated ones, thus reducing investment and increasing the growth marketing ROI

- Multiple micro-channels mapped with the Target Audience are better than a single macro-channel with no TA focus

- It is easier to target the right user segment with micro-channels VS paying for targeting on Facebook or other larger channels

- A new or offbeat channel probably has loopholes that Growth Marketers can leverage compared to a mature channel

A few questions to help create the **channel personas** business are as follows:

- Q1. What kind of problem would the channel solve for a similar target audience as yours?

- Q2. What are the other interests of your target audience? Where do people with similar interests hang out online?

- Q3. What are some of the other brands, products, or tools your audience follows on social media?

- Q5. What are the new channels which have been trending on Google Play or the App Store for the past few weeks?

- Q6. What are the new communities or networks on ProductHunt or BetaList?

- Q7. Which platforms and marketplaces have recently received PR or funding?

- Q8. Which tools or networks are review bloggers in my network also writing about?

Though this is not an exhaustive list, it will give you an understanding of how to come up with growth marketing experiments.

Phase 3: EXPERIMENT

The next phase is the execution or experimentation phase.

The steps in the experimentation phase include:

- Shortlisting ideas (from the Ideation phase we discussed in the previous chapter) and moving them to the experiments list

- Defining the duration of each experiment test which will be the initial cycle of execution

- Ranking the experiments in order of priority – usually using a framework like the ICE score to do this however, I have personally stopped using the ICE score and I use the SPICE score instead

- Decide a success score for each experiment that will help us decide if it is successful or not

- Execute the experiment initial cycle

- Analyse the success score at the end of the test cycle

The Experimentation Phase is where all the hustle happens.

At Mapplinks, I usually assign a **team of 3 people** for each execution cycle. We keep our execution cycles up to 45 days per growth marketing experiment. The team is put together based on the requirements of the experiment.

The team is also assigned so we have the right marketing, tech, copy, and analyst skills as needed. T-shaped marketers are selected based on the level of skill needed for the experiment.

The execution review happens daily and the reporting happens weekly.

Each week, we discuss how the OMTM is improving.

For example, here is a screenshot from the **weekly OMTM tracking** for an influencer outreach campaign and the ratios we measure:

A	B	C	D
Total output	294		
Week 1			
OMTM	# influencer data collected	Total data collected	
Total output	143	**437**	
Week 3			
OMTM	# influencers agreed for collab		
Total output	51		
Week 4			
OMTM	# influencers agreed for collab	Total influencers agreed	Ratio #1: Influencers Agreed/ Data Collected. (%)
Total output	60	**111**	**25**
Week 5			
OMTM	# successful collabs		
Total output	26		
Week 6			
OMTM	# successful collabs		
Total output	22		
Week 7			
OMTM	# successful collabs	Total success collabs	Ratio #2: Success Collabs/ Influencers Agreed (%)
Total output	43	**91**	**81.98**

Figure 1: Growth Marketing Experiment Weekly Analytics

During all the weekly review sessions, adjustments are made to the experiments to improve results and fine-tune the process.

It is essential to review data often in this phase as the initial experiment cycle is the most important one to make future decisions.

As you have observed, Analytics is not a separate phase in Growth Marketing but a process that is put into practice in each phase of Growth Marketing.

Phase 4: SCALE

Once the execution phase is complete, we will have data and learnings to move to the next steps of the growth experiments.

The execution results will tell what worked well and what did not.

What we are looking for at this stage is to take things that work together and scale them.

I also call this the Integration phase. It could be:

1. Integration of the experiment execution cycles within the business process

2. Or Integration in terms of putting together a scaling process to repeat and get more results from the growth campaign further.

Integration or Scaling, in general, is defined as the process of combining different elements in a more effective way.

The combination for us could be:

1. Successful experiments + More manpower

2. Successful experiments + More budgets

3. Successful experiments + Scale with tech

4. Successful experiments + Business processes

The exact steps in this phase would hence differ based on how we decide to Integrate the experiment. However, they would usually include the following:

- Creating a blueprint system of the successful experiment

- Assigning a team to study the blueprint

- Deciding repetition frequency and budgets against ROI

- Using tech to scale the components of the system that can be automated

- Integrating the blueprint into your business process

Important points to note:

- Integration includes the Scaling phase as a part of it and the new Integration phase has a scope much bigger than just scaling and automation.

- Note that Analytics is not a separate phase in the process but a part of each phase. Analytics starts from Day 1 of growth marketing and continues until Integration and beyond.

- Post Integration, you can go back to the idea bank (option 1) or go back to the research phase (option 2) if there have been major changes to the data collection.

Those 4 phases, repeated over time, are what make companies grow.

Chapter 6

How to Conduct Research for Growth

In the previous chapter, we discussed the 10 questions to ask the business or startup to conduct research.

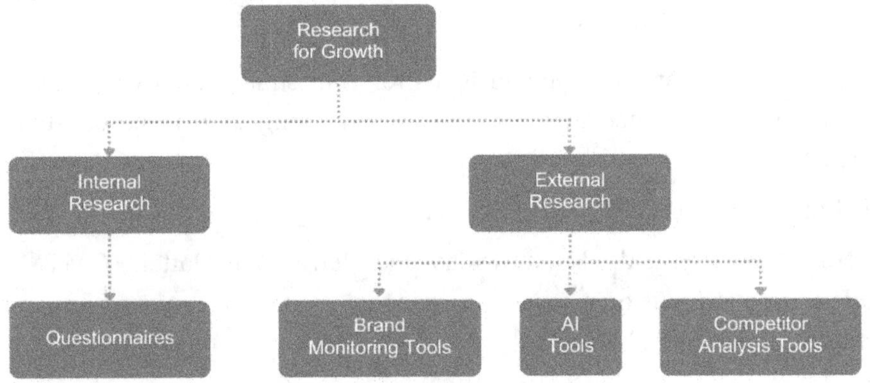

The Research Questionnaire

The 10 questions are listed below:

- What is your north star metric? (6-month goal)
- What is your OMTM? (30-day goal)
- What is your current strategy to reach your goals?
- Describe your ideal target persona
- What is your top value proposition?
- What channels are you currently using to reach your audience?
- What is your current offer and how is it doing in terms of conversions?
- Who are your top 3 competitors?
- What are the communities or other channels your target audience is active on?
- What data do you have from your past campaigns?

These questions can capture data that are internal to the startup.

I came up with these questions after planning growth marketing campaigns for 50+ startups and constantly improving my own growth marketing process.

If you are interested in why I choose these questions, here you go:

What is your north star metric? (6-month goal)

Identifying a north star metric helps define the ultimate goal for your growth marketing efforts.

It provides a clear direction and focus for your strategy, allowing you to align your tactics and initiatives towards achieving significant long-term growth.

What is your OMTM? (30-day goal)

Setting a 30-day goal, also known as One Metric That Matters (OMTM), allows you to focus on a specific metric that has the most impact on your immediate growth objectives.

It helps you prioritize your efforts and measure short-term progress.

What is your current strategy to reach your goals?

Understanding your current growth strategy enables you to assess its effectiveness and identify areas for improvement.

It provides insights into the tactics and channels you are utilizing and helps you evaluate their alignment with your goals.

Describe your ideal target persona

Defining your ideal target persona is crucial for effective targeting and messaging.

It helps you understand your audience's needs, preferences, and pain points, allowing you to tailor your marketing efforts to resonate with them effectively.

What is your top value proposition?

Your value proposition is what sets you apart from your competitors and convinces customers to choose your product or service.

Clearly defining and understanding your top value proposition helps you craft compelling messages and positioning that resonates with your target audience.

What channels are you currently using to reach your audience?

Identifying the channels, you are currently using provides insights into your existing marketing reach and allows you to evaluate their performance.

It helps you assess if you are utilizing the most effective channels for reaching your target audience and informs future channel selection.

What is your current offer and how is it doing in terms of conversions?

Assessing your current offer's performance in terms of conversions helps you gauge its effectiveness in driving customer actions.

It enables you to optimize your offer based on data-driven insights and improve conversion rates.

Who are your top 3 competitors?

Understanding your top competitors is essential for competitive analysis and differentiation.

It allows you to identify their strengths and weaknesses, benchmark your performance against theirs, and uncover opportunities for differentiation and improvement.

What are the communities or other channels your target audience is active on?

Identifying the communities and channels where your target audience is active helps you expand your reach and engage with them effectively.

It allows you to discover new marketing channels and strategies to connect with your audience where they are most receptive.

What data do you have from your past campaigns?

Analysing past campaign data provides valuable insights into what has worked and what has not.

It helps you identify trends, patterns, and success factors, allowing you to refine your growth marketing strategies based on proven data-driven insights.

Research Questionnaire Examples

If you are thinking about what kind of answers you can expect to get with these questions, here are 3 examples from different kinds of businesses:

Question	B2B Digital Agency	B2C Ecommerce	Consumer Mobile App
1. What is your north star metric? (6-month goal)	Increase monthly recurring revenue (MRR) by 30%	Achieve a 20% growth in online sales revenue	Reach 1 million active users
2. What is your OMTM? (30-day goal)	Increase website conversion rate by 15%	Boost average order value by 10%	Improve daily active user (DAU) retention rate by 20%
3. What is your current strategy to reach your goals?	Focus on inbound lead generation through content marketing and SEO	Implement targeted social media advertising campaigns and personalized email marketing	Enhance user onboarding experience and implement referral program
4. Describe your ideal target persona	Small to medium-sized businesses seeking digital marketing services	Tech-savvy millennials interested in trendy fashion and lifestyle products	Gen Z mobile users passionate about fitness and wellness

5. What is your top value proposition?	Customized digital strategies that drive measurable results and ROI	High-quality products at competitive prices with fast shipping	Convenient and intuitive mobile app for tracking workouts and personalized fitness plans
6. What channels are you currently using to reach your audience?	LinkedIn, industry-specific forums, webinars, and networking events	Facebook, Instagram, Google Ads, email marketing	App Store optimization (ASO), social media platforms, influencer partnerships
7. What offer are you currently offering and how is it doing in terms of conversions?	Free website audit and consultation, with a 20% conversion rate	Limited-time discounts and free shipping, resulting in a 15% conversion rate	Freemium model with in-app purchases, leading to a 10% conversion rate
8. Who are your top 3 competitors?	Competitor A: Leading digital agency with expertise in SEO	Competitor B: Well-established online marketplace with a wide product range	Competitor C: Popular mobile app for tracking fitness activities and workouts
9. What are the communities or other channels your target audience is active on?	Digital marketing forums, LinkedIn groups, and industry-specific online communities	Social media platforms (Facebook, Instagram, Pinterest), fashion blogs, and online forums	Fitness and wellness communities, health-focused social media groups

10. What past data do you have from your past campaigns?	Conversion rates from previous lead generation campaigns, customer acquisition cost (CAC), and customer lifetime value (CLV)	Conversion rates from previous promotional campaigns, customer retention rate, and average order value (AOV)	User acquisition metrics, retention rates, and in-app engagement data

Research Using Tools

The second part of research that can open our world to new ideas and opportunities is external research, outside of the startup's own data.

For this part of the research, we can use various tools.

I have listed the top tools I have used to conduct research for multiple clients.

SimilarWeb

SimilarWeb is a powerful tool for gaining insights into competitors, audience behaviour, and traffic sources.

By analysing website traffic, engagement metrics, and search keywords, SimilarWeb provides valuable information for benchmarking, identifying growth opportunities, and understanding target audience interests.

ChatGPT

ChatGPT can assist in generating experiment ideas, conducting content research, and analysing audience preferences.

By engaging in conversational interactions with ChatGPT, marketers can uncover valuable insights to inform their growth strategies.

SEMRush

SEMRush offers features for competitor analysis, keyword research, backlink analysis, and more.

With SEMRush, growth marketers can gain a deeper understanding of competitors' strategies, identify high-performing keywords, and optimize their SEO efforts.

Ahrefs

Ahrefs provides valuable insights into backlinks, organic keywords, and content performance.

By leveraging Ahrefs, growth marketers can identify link-building opportunities, conduct in-depth competitor analysis, and optimize their content strategy.

Brand24

Brand24 allows growth marketers to monitor brand mentions, track social media conversations, and analyse sentiment around their brand.

By staying updated on customer feedback and market trends, marketers can make informed decisions and identify opportunities for growth.

Facebook Ads Library

The Facebook Ads Library provides transparency into the advertising strategies of competitors and industry leaders.

Marketers can explore ad creatives, targeting options, and performance metrics to gain inspiration for their own campaigns.

Using this, growth marketers can learn from proven strategies and improve their advertising efforts.

BuzzSumo

BuzzSumo is a content research tool that helps identify popular content, trending topics, and influential industry leaders.

Using BuzzSumo, growth marketers can gain insights into audience preferences and develop content ideas that resonate with their target market.

AnswerThePublic

AnswerThePublic is a valuable tool for understanding customer questions and search trends.

It provides visualizations of frequently asked questions related to specific keywords, helping growth marketers identify content gaps and create relevant, informative content that addresses audience needs.

BuiltWith

BuiltWith allows growth marketers to gain insights into the technology stack and website trends of their competitors.

It provides information about the CMS platforms, plugins, and analytics tools that competitors are using.

This can be used for tech analysis as well as a lead generation database.

The research phase of the growth marketing process is critical for generating experiment ideas and uncovering valuable insights. These insights will inform data-driven decision making and drive impactful growth experiments. Remember, research is an iterative process and continuous improvement in research techniques will lead to more successful growth strategies.

In the next chapter, we will explore the ideation phase, where we will turn research insights into actionable experiment ideas.

Chapter 7

How to Generate Growth Ideas

The best place to start with ideas is from the research.

If you have done your research well (as per the previous chapter), you would naturally have a huge list of growth ideas.

But there are more sources of idea generation.

We will go through 4 sources:

1. The Growth Research Questionnaire
2. The Growth Research Tools
3. The 3Cs framework
4. The 3Ps framework

Ideas from the Research Questionnaire

Here is an example of how the 10 growth research questions can lead to ideas:

Research Question	Response	Growth Idea
What is your north star metric? (6-month goal)	Increase monthly active users from 10,000 to 50,000	Implement a referral program to incentivize user acquisition
What is your OMTM? (30-day goal)	Increase conversion rate on website by 20%	A/B test website landing page variations
What is your current strategy to reach your goals?	Focus on content marketing and social media advertising	Explore influencer partnerships to amplify reach

Describe your ideal target persona	Health-conscious individuals aged 25-40, working professionals	Create targeted content for busy professionals
What is your top value proposition?	Personalized workout plans and real-time progress tracking	Highlight unique features in marketing campaigns
What channels are you currently using to reach your audience?	Instagram, Facebook, Google Ads, and email marketing	Experiment with YouTube fitness tutorials
What offer are you currently offering and how is it performing in terms of conversions?	30-day free trial with a 20% conversion rate	Introduce a limited-time discount to increase conversions
Who are your top 3 competitors?	FitFusion, Sweatflix, FitnessFlow	Analyse competitor offerings and differentiate
What are the communities or other channels your target audience is active on?	Fitness forums, Reddit communities, and health-related blogs	Engage with communities through content contributions
What past data do you have from your past campaigns?	Average customer acquisition cost: $15, Lifetime value: $100	Optimize advertising budget allocation based on LTV

In the above example, I have only shown one idea from each of the research questions.

When we run the questionnaire, you should end up with 2-3 great ideas from each question, and many other good ideas.

Ideas from Tools

Next, let us look at how you can find ideas from the research tools we used in the previous chapter.

Research Tool	Growth Ideas
SimilarWeb	Explore partnerships with popular fitness websites and blogs to drive traffic and referrals
ChatGPT	Create engaging and informative fitness-related articles and posts to attract and educate the target audience
SEMRush	Optimize website content and create targeted blog posts around popular fitness keywords to improve organic search rankings
Ahrefs	Reach out to websites with relevant fitness content for guest blogging opportunities and backlink exchanges
Brand24	Respond to customer feedback and reviews promptly, and leverage positive mentions for social proof and testimonials
Facebook Ads Library	Develop compelling ad creatives and messages highlighting the unique value proposition of the fitness startup
BuzzSumo	Create shareable and informative fitness videos, infographics, or blog posts that align with the trending topics in the industry
AnswerThePublic	Create a series of educational videos or blog posts that address frequently asked questions about fitness and health
Google Analytics	Identify pages with high bounce rates and optimize them to improve user engagement and conversion rates
BuiltWith	Explore new marketing and analytics tools used by competitors to enhance the startup's marketing capabilities

You can see some generic ways to implement growth ideas based on the tools.

I have included Google Analytics in this list as it is a huge database of growth ideas, just waiting for you to unpack them!

Well, this is just the start of generating ideas.

Next, let me share 2 key frameworks I use for ideation.

I use the 3Cs framework and 3Ps framework to generate new growth hacking ideas and new marketing ideas for startups and businesses.

And it has been one of the most effective ways I have been able to generate a huge list of new ideas in bulk.

The 3Cs Framework

The 3Cs stand for:

- C – Channels
- C – Competitor
- C – Communities

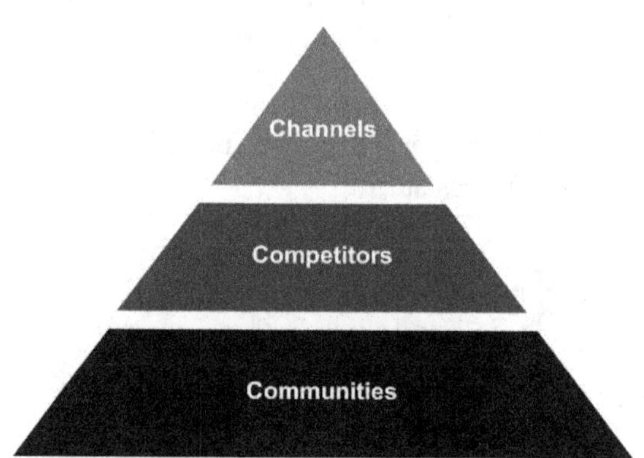

The 3Cs of Growth Hacking

Here is how to use it:

Step 1: Channels – Make a list of all the channels where the target audience is active.

This is similar to what most digital marketers usually do. The next 2 steps are more unique to growth hacking.

Step 2: Competitors – Once you understand your target persona, make a list of all the competitors (include direct competitors and audience competitors)

P.S. Audience competitors may not be providing the same solution or solving the same problem as your startup but they would be targeting the same audience.

Step 3: Communities – Find all the comments where the target audience has discussions or posts.

Once you have this list of the 3Cs, you can then start ideation how you can tap into them.

There are different ways to leverage the 3Cs in growth hacking and growth marketing.

The framework we can use here to find how to leverage the 3Cs is the 3Ps framework of growth hacking.

The 3Ps Framework

And the 3Ps stand for:

- P – Piggybacking
- P – Partnerships
- P – Paid Opportunities

The 3Ps of Growth Hacking

Here are the 3Ps:

- **Piggybacking** – Finding ways to enter the target channel or competitor or community and move the audience from there into your funnel

- **Partnerships** – Explore collaboration opportunities

- **Paid Opportunities** – Find paid targeting options in the target 3Cs where you can run ads or sponsorships on them

I suggest the startups I consult to execute in the same order.

Step 1: Piggybacking – Try to execute growth hacks first where you can piggyback and leverage the OPNs of the 3Cs

Step 2: Partnerships – If piggybacking fails or if piggybacking is successful and you find opportunities to create a partnership, go ahead and reach out to the target channel, competitors, or community for an organic partnership.

Step 3: Paid Opportunities – If none of the above work, use the money. If you do not get a good deal, then go back to your list of 3Cs and repeat the 3P framework with another channel, competitor, or community.

Growth hackers usually follow the order Piggybacking > Partnerships > Paid vs Digital marketers who might follow Paid > Partnerships (piggybacking is a growth hacking skill).

You can choose to follow the order as per your analysis of the particular target. Sometimes, it is easier to get into a partnership than piggybacking when both you and the target have aligned interests.

And in some cases, it could even be cheaper to explore a paid opportunity than run scripts, hacks, scraping, or other workflows for piggybacking.

You can adjust your strategy based on the specific case but in general, the 3Cs and 3Ps frameworks are extremely useful and handy tools for growth hacking ideation.

Here is an example of how you can map the 3Cs and 3Ps together to create growth marketing ideas:

	Channels	**Competitors**	**Communities**
Piggybacking	Collaborate with popular blogs and social media platforms related to the target audience's interests	Leverage partnerships with complementary products or services	Engage with online communities focused on specific interests
Partnerships	Establish partnerships with complementary businesses or influencers to reach their customer base	Collaborate with industry influencers or thought leaders	Form alliances with related businesses or influencers to tap into their existing customer base
Paid Opportunities	Run targeted ads on relevant platforms or publications to reach the target audience	Sponsor relevant events or platforms	Advertise on relevant platforms or publications to reach the target audience

This is how growth marketers come up with a framework for generating ideas. I created the 3Cs and 3Ps to include all the various combinations of ideas you can generate.

With the above 4 methods (questionnaires, tools, and 3Cs 3Ps frameworks), you will be able to have enough ideas to test and iterate in your growth marketing journey.

Build Your Ideas Database

(Beginners can skip this section for now)

As you run growth experiments, you can build your own database of growth ideas.

Remember not to rely too much on idea lists you find online as what has worked before may not work any longer. Also, what works for one startup may not work for another.

Instead, it is better to rely on your own past data as you can map your ideas that worked for a specific startup in the past.

In future, if you work with similar ideas, you can test those ideas again in new experiments.

Here is a simple three-step process to help you create and maintain your growth ideas database:

Step 1: Document and Capture Growth Ideas

The first step is to document and capture all your growth ideas as they come to you or your team. This can be done through brainstorming sessions, individual contributions, competitor analysis, customer feedback, or insights from industry research.

Make sure to capture the following information for each growth idea:

- **Brief Description:** Summarize the growth idea in a concise manner.

- **Objective:** Clearly define the goal or problem the growth idea aims to address.

- **Target Metric:** Identify the specific metric that you expect to impact with the growth idea.

- **Channels/Platforms:** Mention the channels or platforms where the growth idea will be implemented.

- **Supporting Data:** Include any supporting data or insights that validate the growth idea.

- **Notes:** Add any additional details or considerations that may be relevant to the growth idea.

Step 2: Conduct Experiments and Collect Results

Once you have a list of growth ideas in your database, it is time to execute them through experiments or tests. Design and implement A/B tests, user surveys, landing page variations, email campaigns, or any other relevant method to validate the growth ideas.

During the experimentation phase, make sure to track and collect data on the following:

- **Test Duration:** Note the duration of the experiment to establish a timeline.

- **Sample Size:** Record the number of participants, visitors, or users involved in the test.

- **Target Metric:** Measure and record the impact of the growth idea on the target metric.

Step 3: Update and Analyse Results in the Database

After completing each experiment, update your growth ideas database with the results and insights gained. Incorporate the following information:

- **Results:** Record the outcomes of the experiments, including the impact on the target metric.

- **Learnings:** Document key learnings, observations, or insights gained from the experiment.

- **Statistical Significance:** Note the level of statistical significance achieved in the test.

- **Recommendations:** Provide recommendations based on the results for future actions or iterations.

- **Next Steps:** Outline the next steps, whether it involves further optimization, additional experiments, or discarding the growth idea.

By following these three steps of documenting, conducting experiments, and updating the results in your growth ideas database, you can create a valuable resource to inform and guide your future growth initiatives.

Chapter 8

How to Execute Growth Experiments

In this chapter, we will go through the process of executing experiments.

Experimentation plays a crucial role in growth marketing, enabling businesses to test hypotheses, validate assumptions, and drive data-backed decision-making. We will delve into the steps involved in experimentation, from measuring and researching to ideating and executing experiments.

Before we start, let us establish the key rules of experiment.

Key Rules for Execution

1. Run growth experiments in sprints of 4-6 weeks
2. Review results each week to adjust the next experiment cycle
3. Do not drop the experiment before 4 weeks unless you have maxed out on your learnings
4. Do not keep extending the experiment if there is no positive movement in the direction of your OMTM at the end of 6 weeks

Let me explain the above in more detail.

Experiment Duration: Run growth experiments in sprints of 4-6 weeks

Set a specific timeframe for each experiment to maintain focus and allow for adequate data collection.

This timeframe provides enough opportunity to test and iterate while also avoiding prolonged experiments that may hinder progress.

Weekly Review and Adjustment: Review results each week to adjust the next experiment cycle

Regularly analyse and evaluate the data collected from the ongoing experiment

Use these weekly reviews to make informed decisions on whether to continue, modify, or terminate the current experiment.

Adjust the next experiment cycle based on the insights gained and lessons learned from the previous week.

Minimum Experiment Duration: Do not drop the experiment before 4 weeks unless you have maxed out on your learnings

Give experiments sufficient time to gather meaningful data and insights.

Avoid prematurely terminating an experiment before the 4-week mark, unless you have already gathered all the relevant learnings and insights.

This ensures that experiments have a fair chance to produce actionable results and avoids cutting them short prematurely.

Maximum Experiment Duration: Do not keep extending the experiment if there is no positive movement in the direction of your OMTM at the end of 6 weeks

Evaluate the progress of the experiment at the end of the 6-week mark.

If the experiment does not show any positive movement towards your One Metric That Matters (OMTM), consider concluding it.

Avoid extending experiments indefinitely if there is no evidence of desired results, as it may consume resources without generating meaningful insights.

Experimentation is a systematic approach that involves several key steps to ensure reliable and actionable results.

F.I.R.E Framework for Experimentation

You can remember the above framework (also) as the F.I.R.E framework:

- **F - Fixed Duration:** Run growth experiments in sprints of 4-6 weeks.

- **I - Iterative Review:** Review results each week to adjust the next experiment cycle.

- **R - Respect Minimum:** Do not drop the experiment before 4 weeks unless you have maxed out on your learnings.
- **E - End if Necessary:** Do not keep extending the experiment if there is no positive movement in the direction of your OMTM at the end of 6 weeks.

Remembering the acronym F.I.R.E. can help you recall the key elements of the framework for running growth experiments effectively and efficiently.

Growth Marketing Process Review

To quickly review where experimentation comes in our growth marketing process, the 4 stages of the growth marketing process are as follows:

Measure: Setting a Baseline and Identifying Key Metrics

Before diving into experiments, it is essential to establish a baseline by measuring your current performance. This baseline serves as a reference point to evaluate the effectiveness of your experiments. Identify key metrics aligned with your growth goals and ensure they are measurable and trackable.

Research: Conducting In-Depth Research for Insights

Thorough research is crucial to gain insights about your target audience, competitors, industry trends, and customer behaviour. Utilize tools like SimilarWeb, SEMRush, Ahrefs, and Facebook Ads Library to gather competitive intelligence and identify potential growth opportunities. Leverage ChatGPT, BuzzSumo, and AnswerThePublic to understand customer needs, pain points, and content preferences.

Ideate: Generating Experiment Ideas and Hypotheses

Based on your research findings, brainstorm experiment ideas that align with your growth objectives. Use a structured approach like the SPICE framework to prioritize ideas.

Execute: Implementing and Running Experiments

Once you have defined your experiment ideas and hypotheses, it is time to execute them. Determine the variables, control groups, and experimental methodology for each experiment. Set up A/B tests, multivariate tests, or split tests to compare different variations. Allocate resources, establish timelines, and implement changes to execute the experiments effectively.

This is where key execution activities come in including resource allocation, data collection, experiment tracking, and weekly reporting and analytics.

Key Tips for Experimentation

Determine Key Variables

Identify the key variables that you will be testing during the experiment. These variables could include different variations of landing pages, email subject lines, pricing structures, ad copy, or any other element that you believe could impact the desired outcome.

By focusing on the key variables, you can isolate their impact on the results and gain meaningful insights.

Define Control Groups

Control groups are essential for measuring the effectiveness of your experiment. They act as a baseline against which you compare the performance of the experimental group.

The control group should remain unaffected by any changes made in the experiment, allowing you to assess the true impact of the variables being tested.

Implement A/B or Split Testing

A/B testing or split testing is a widely used methodology in growth marketing experiments. It involves dividing your audience into two or more groups and exposing each group to different variations of the experiment.

This enables you to compare the performance of the variations and identify which one yields the desired results.

Allocate Resources

Ensure you have the necessary resources in place to execute the experiment effectively. This includes allocating budget, manpower, and technology needed to implement the changes and collect data.

Consider any dependencies or technical requirements to ensure a smooth execution process.

Establish a Timeline

Set a clear timeline for your experiment, including the start and end dates. It is important to give the experiment sufficient time to gather meaningful data while also ensuring it does not drag on indefinitely.

By setting a timeline, you can stay organized, track progress, and make informed decisions about continuing or concluding the experiment.

Monitor and Measure

During the experiment, closely monitor the performance metrics you identified in the measure phase. Continuously collect data and analyse the results to understand how the variations are performing.

Use analytics tools like Google Analytics or any other relevant tracking tools to measure and track key metrics accurately.

Document and Learn

Record every detail of your experiment, including the variables tested, the implementation process, and the outcomes observed.

Documentation allows you to refer back to the experiment later, analyse the results, and draw insights.

It also helps in sharing learnings with the team, facilitating knowledge transfer, and avoiding repetition of unsuccessful experiments.

I personally use Loom to keep a recording of my experimentation. You can also use a simple doc or Google sheets.

Analyse and Draw Insights

Once the experiment is complete, analyse the data collected and draw meaningful insights. Compare the performance of the experimental group against the control group and identify any statistically significant differences.

Evaluate the impact of the variables tested and assess their influence on the desired outcome. These insights will guide future decision-making and further experimentation.

I personally use a weekly cycle to make quick adjustments to the experiments based on data.

This leads to the discussion on using lean and agile principles for execution.

Using Lean & Agile Principles for Experimentation

You can follow the blueprint below to stay lean and go agile with your experiment execution:

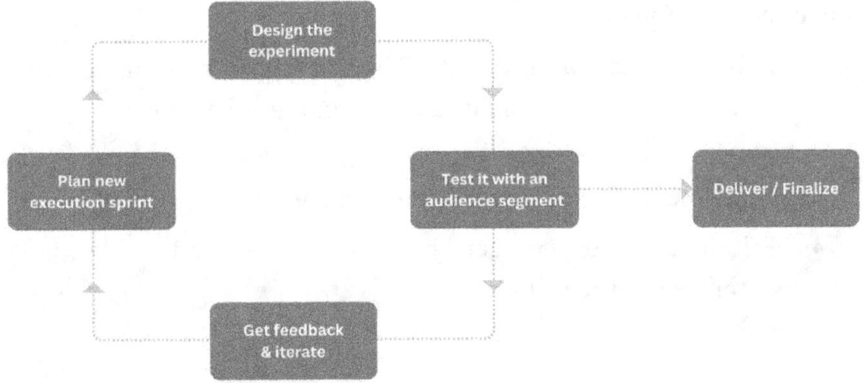

Designing the Experiment

- Apply lean principles to design experiments that are focused, resource-efficient, and aligned with your growth goals.

- Clearly define the hypothesis, variables, and expected outcomes of the experiment.

- Keep the experiment scope manageable to minimize waste and maximize learning.

Testing it with an Audience Segment

- Take an agile approach by testing the experiment with a specific audience segment.

- This allows you to gather feedback and insights from a targeted group and make quick iterations based on their responses.

- By focusing on smaller segments, you can iterate faster and refine your experiment before scaling to a larger audience.

Deliver & Measure

- Once the experiment has been tested and refined, finalize the implementation.

- Ensure all necessary changes are in place and any technical requirements are met.

- Double-check tracking and measurement tools to accurately capture data during the experiment.

New Execution Sprint

- Following the lean and agile principles, plan the next execution sprint based on the insights gained from the experiment.

- Identify new experiment ideas or modifications to existing experiments for continuous improvement.

- Prioritize the experiments based on impact and feasibility to optimize resource allocation.

Chapter 9
A/B Testing for Growth

Introduction to A/B Testing for Growth Marketers

A/B testing, also known as split testing, is a powerful method of experimentation used to determine which version of a variable has the most impact on target business metrics.

It plays a vital role in Conversion Rate Optimization (CRO) by improving overall conversion rates and addressing user pain points. By eliminating guesswork and relying on data, A/B testing allows marketers to make informed decisions and drive continuous improvement in conversion rates.

Understanding A/B Testing and Its Benefits

A/B testing is highly regarded for its numerous benefits in the field of CRO:

- **Data-Driven Decision Making:** A/B testing brings in data and eliminates guesswork, enabling marketers to make decisions based on actual results rather than assumptions.

- **Improved Conversion Rates:** By identifying winning variations through A/B tests, businesses can optimize their marketing elements and enhance their conversion rates.

- **Lean and Incremental Changes:** A/B testing follows a lean process, making small and incremental changes to avoid significant risks to conversion rates.

- **Agility and Feedback Integration:** A/B testing allows businesses to reach their target audience, gather feedback, and iterate at any time, ensuring an agile approach to optimization.

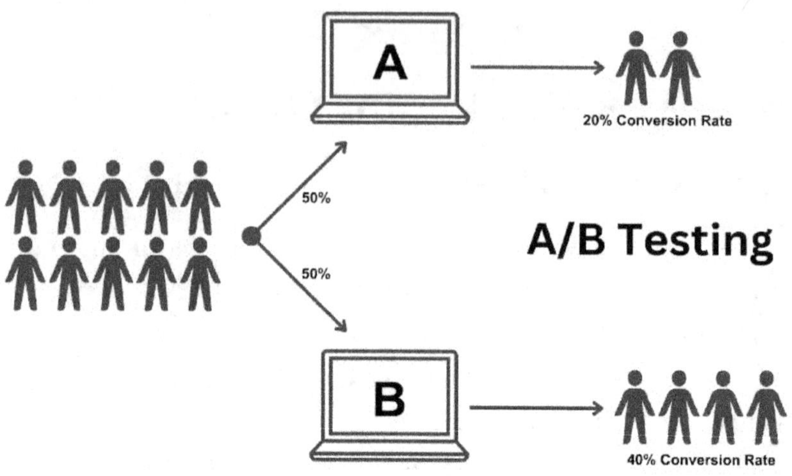

Key Terms and Definitions in A/B Testing

Before delving further into A/B testing, it is essential to understand some key terms:

- **Control:** The original version that serves as a baseline for comparison.

- **Variation:** The new version being tested against the control.

- **Winner:** The version that demonstrates positive movement in the target metrics.

- **Target Metric:** The specific metric measured to determine the winner of the A/B test.

- **Lift/Drop:** The increase or decrease in the target metrics compared to the control.

- **Hypothesis:** The rationale behind conducting the A/B test.

- **Sample Size:** The number of visitors or traffic included in the test, affecting the test's accuracy and variability.

- **Variance:** The average variability in the data points, influencing the accuracy of the mean.

- **Statistical Significance:** The measure of how significant the test results are and whether they reflect true differences or are due to chance.

- **Segmentation:** The process of dividing the audience into distinct groups based on specific characteristics to analyse the performance of variations across different segments.

- **Conversion Rate:** The percentage of visitors or users who complete a desired action, such as making a purchase or signing up for a newsletter.

- **Click-Through Rate (CTR):** The percentage of people who click on a specific element, such as a button or link, compared to the total number of views or impressions.

- **Bounce Rate:** The percentage of visitors who leave a webpage without interacting with it or navigating to any other page on the same website.

- **Multivariate Testing:** A form of testing where multiple variations of different elements are tested simultaneously to determine the most effective combination.

- **Confidence Interval:** The range of values within which the true effect of the variation is likely to fall with a certain level of confidence.

- **Significance Level:** The predetermined threshold used to determine whether the results of the A/B test are statistically significant. It is commonly set at 0.05 or 0.01.

- **Segmentation:** The process of dividing the audience into distinct groups based on specific characteristics to analyse the performance of variations across different segments.

- **Split Testing:** Another term for A/B testing, where two or more variations are compared to determine the best-performing option.

- **Randomization:** The process of assigning visitors or users randomly to either the control or variation group to minimize bias and ensure equal distribution.

- **Sample Bias:** A bias that occurs when the sample used in the A/B test is not representative of the target audience, leading to inaccurate results.

- **Data Integrity:** Ensuring the accuracy, completeness, and reliability of the data collected during the A/B test.

- **Learning Effect:** The potential impact of repeated exposure to a variation on users' behaviour and response, which may skew the test results.

With these terms, you will be able to understand A/B experiments and reports better.

Identifying Elements for A/B Testing

While it is tempting to A/B test everything, it is crucial to prioritize elements and channels that have a higher impact.

Here are some examples of elements that can be A/B tested within various channels:

- Copy on ads and landing pages
- Colors on ad creatives and landing page banners
- CTA button texts and colors
- Form fields on landing pages
- Subject lines on emailers
- Price points on product pages
- Order of content on landing pages
- Timing of sending on emailers and posting on social media
- Media formats and content style on social media
- CTAs on blog posts

Types of A/B Tests

There are three main types of A/B tests:

- **Split Tests:** These tests compare fundamentally different designs or versions, focusing on significant variations in elements. They are ideal for testing large-scale changes.

- **Multivariate Tests:** In this method, multiple variations of different elements are tested simultaneously, allowing for efficient testing of multiple combinations. The number of variants increases exponentially with the number of elements being tested.

- **Multipage Tests:** This type of test allows changes to be tested across multiple pages or assets, maintaining a consistent user experience throughout a funnel or user journey.

Statistical Approaches to A/B Testing

Two primary statistical approaches are commonly used in A/B testing:

- **Frequentist Approach:** This approach determines probabilities based on how frequently an event occurs with multiple trials or data points. It requires a large sample size and can be more time-consuming and expensive.

- **Bayesian Approach:** This approach calculates probabilities based on prior knowledge and updates them as new data becomes available. It requires a smaller sample size and allows for more flexibility in decision-making.

Key Steps in Conducting an A/B Test

1. **Define the Objective:** Clearly articulate the goal of the A/B test and the specific metric you want to improve.

2. **Formulate a Hypothesis:** Develop a hypothesis that explains the expected impact of the variation on the target metric.

3. **Determine Sample Size:** Calculate the required sample size to achieve statistically significant results. Consider factors such as expected effect size, desired statistical power, and acceptable level of significance.

4. **Create Control and Variation Versions:** Develop the control version (original) and the variation version (modified) that will be tested against each other.

5. **Randomly Assign Visitors:** Randomly allocate visitors to the control and variation groups to minimize bias and ensure a fair comparison.

6. **Run the Experiment:** Implement the A/B test by displaying the control and variation versions to their respective groups simultaneously.

7. **Gather Data:** Collect relevant data on the target metric from both the control and variation groups.

8. **Analyse Results:** Use statistical analysis to determine the significance of the results and calculate the lift or drop in the target metric.

9. **Draw Conclusions:** Based on the analysis, determine whether the variation version outperformed the control version and draw actionable insights from the results.

10. **Implement Winning Variation:** If the variation version is determined to be the winner, implement it as the new control version and continue optimizing.

Best Practices for A/B Testing

To ensure effective A/B testing and reliable results, consider the following best practices:

- **Test One Variable at a Time:** Focus on testing a single variable in each A/B test to clearly identify its impact on the target metric.

- **Define a Clear Conversion Goal:** Clearly define the primary conversion goal and ensure it aligns with the objective of the A/B test.

- **Prioritize High-Impact Elements:** Prioritize elements that have a high potential impact on conversion rates to maximize the effectiveness of the A/B test.

- **Sufficient Sample Size:** Ensure an adequate sample size to achieve statistically significant results and reduce the likelihood of false positives or false negatives.

- **Run Tests for Sufficient Duration:** Allow A/B tests to run for a sufficient duration to account for different user behaviours and avoid drawing conclusions too early.

- **Consider Segmentation:** Segment your audience to perform A/B tests on specific user segments and understand how different variations impact different user groups.

- **Monitor External Factors:** Be aware of external factors that could influence the test results and consider controlling for them or accounting for their impact.

- **Document and Learn:** Maintain documentation of A/B test results, learnings, and insights to inform future optimization efforts and build institutional knowledge.

A/B testing is a valuable technique for growth marketers as it allows businesses to optimize their marketing elements, enhance conversion rates, and make data-driven decisions.

By following best practices, prioritizing high-impact elements, and analysing results statistically, businesses can continuously improve their conversion rates and drive growth. Remember to iterate, learn from each test, and apply the insights gained to future experiments to foster a culture of optimization and improvement.

A/B tests can be very simple changes and do not have to be highly technical.

Here are some examples of startups where we conducted A/B tests and the kinds of results achieved:

Startup	Industry	A/B Test	Results
TechBuzz	Technology	Button Color: Red vs. Green	Green button resulted in a 20% increase in CTR
Fashionista	Fashion	Call-to-Action Text: "Buy Now" vs. "Shop Now"	Shop Now text led to a 15% increase in conversions
FitTrack	Health & Fitness	Pricing Page Layout: Vertical vs. Horizontal	Horizontal layout increased engagement by 25%
FoodLicious	Food & Beverage	Product Image: Single vs. Multiple	Multiple images led to a 10% higher conversion rate
TravelMate	Travel	Headline Copy: Descriptive vs. Emotive	Emotive headline resulted in a 30% uplift in CTR
FinTechPro	Finance	Call-to-Action Placement: Above vs. Below Fold	Above-fold placement generated 25% more conversions
PetPaws	Pet Care	Free Shipping Threshold: $50 vs. $75	$75 threshold increased average order value by 15%
HomeRevamp	Home Decor	Product Descriptions: Short vs. Long	Long descriptions led to a 12% higher conversion rate
EduMinds	Education	Video Placement: Top vs. Bottom	Top placement resulted in a 20% increase in video views

ArtistryCrafts	Arts & Crafts	Image Background: White vs. Colored	Colored background led to a 15% higher engagement

As you can see, small changes can lead to incremental results.

The results can further be compounded as you layer A/B tests on top of each other in either different stages of the funnel OR throughout time.

ArtistryCrafts	Arts & Crafts	Image Background: White vs. Colored	Colored background led to a 15% higher engagement

Chapter 10

Boost Conversions with CRO Experiments

Introduction to Conversion Rate Optimization (CRO)

Conversion Rate Optimization (CRO) is a crucial aspect of growth marketing that focuses on improving the effectiveness of your conversion funnel to maximize conversions and achieve business goals.

By conducting CRO experiments, businesses can identify barriers to conversion, optimize user experience, and drive significant improvements in their conversion rates. In this chapter, we will explore the key strategies and techniques to boost conversions through CRO experiments.

Understanding the Conversion Funnel

To effectively optimize conversions, it is essential to understand the different stages of the conversion funnel. From initial awareness to the final conversion action, each stage presents unique challenges and opportunities.

By analysing user behaviour and identifying conversion bottlenecks, businesses can prioritize their CRO efforts and allocate resources strategically to improve conversions at each stage.

Conversion Funnel: Ecommerce Example

Here is an example of an ecommerce store and the stages of the conversion funnel based on the user journey:

Stage 1: Product Discovery

In this stage, users discover your ecommerce store and the products you offer. They might find your store through search engines, social media, online ads, or word of mouth. The goal at this stage is to capture their attention and pique their interest in your products.

Stage 2: Landing on Product Pages

Once users are aware of your ecommerce store, they will land on specific product pages. These pages provide detailed information about the product, including images, descriptions, pricing, and customer reviews. The goal at this stage is to engage users and make them interested enough to consider purchasing the product.

Stage 3: Adding to Cart

When users find a product they like, they have the option to add it to their shopping cart. This action indicates their intent to purchase. At this stage, it is essential to make the cart adding process seamless and user-friendly. Clear calls-to-action and an intuitive interface can help encourage users to proceed to the next stage.

Stage 4: Checkout Process2

Once users have added products to their cart, they proceed to the checkout process. This stage involves entering shipping and billing information, selecting payment methods, and reviewing the order details. The goal is to provide a smooth and hassle-free checkout experience to minimize cart abandonment and maximize conversions.

Stage 5: Order Confirmation

After users successfully complete the checkout process, they receive an order confirmation. This confirmation serves as a reassurance that their purchase has been processed successfully. It is an opportunity to thank them for their order, provide relevant details such as shipping timelines, and encourage them to keep exploring your store or share their purchase on social media.

Stage 6: Post-Purchase Experience

The post-purchase stage is often overlooked but plays a crucial role in customer satisfaction and potential repeat purchases. Providing exceptional customer service, order tracking updates, personalized recommendations, and requesting feedback are essential components of this stage. By nurturing the post-purchase experience, you can encourage customer loyalty and advocacy.

Each stage of the conversion funnel requires careful optimization to maximize conversions and improve the overall user experience. By understanding the user journey and implementing effective strategies at each stage, ecommerce stores can increase their conversion rates and drive growth.

At each stage, you will have a conversion rate from that stage to the next stage.

For example, at the "Product Discovery" stage, you may have a conversion rate of 20%, meaning that out of every 100 users who discover your ecommerce store, 20 proceed to the next stage and land on product pages.

Moving to the next stage, let us say you have a conversion rate of 40% from "Product Pages" to "Adding to Cart."

This means that out of the 20 users who landed on product pages, 8 of them add the product to their cart.

As users progress to the "Checkout Process" stage, you might have a conversion rate of 70%.

So out of the 8 users who added products to their cart, 5 of them proceed to the checkout process.

Continuing further, let us assume a conversion rate of 80% from the "Checkout Process" to "Order Confirmation."

This means that out of the 5 users in the checkout process, 4 of them successfully complete the purchase and receive the order confirmation.

Finally, at the "Post-Purchase Experience" stage, you may have a conversion rate of 60% in terms of encouraging customers to provide feedback or make a repeat purchase.

Out of the 4 users who completed a purchase, 2 of them provide feedback or become repeat customers.

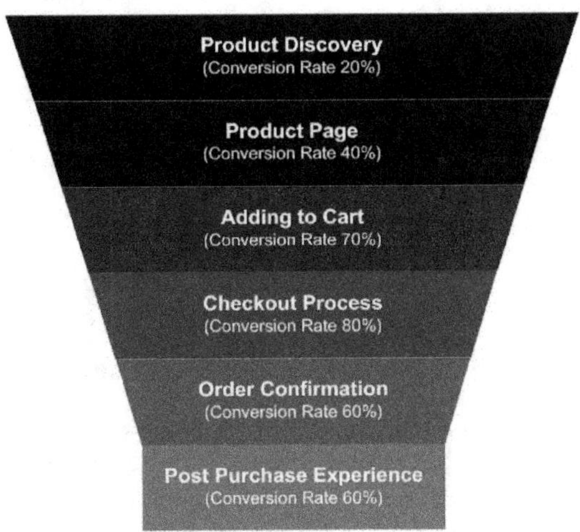

These conversion rates provide insights into the effectiveness of each stage in the conversion funnel.

By tracking and optimizing these rates, you can identify areas of improvement and implement strategies to increase conversions at each stage.

Here is an ecommerce example of the various CRO experiments you can run in each stage and micro-stage of the conversion funnel:

Customer Journey Stage	CRO Experiment
Homepage	Testing different hero images and messaging
Category Page	Implementing filter options and sorting mechanisms
Product Listing	A/B testing product titles and descriptions
Product Page	1. Variations in product images and zoom functionality, 2. A/B testing product pricing and discounts, 3. Testing different product videos or demos
Add to Cart	1. Implementing one-step vs. multi-step checkout process, 2. Testing various call-to-action buttons for adding to cart

Checkout	1. Simplifying the checkout form fields, 2. Testing progress indicators for multi-step checkout
Payment Processing	1. A/B testing payment options and methods, 2. Implementing trust signals and security badges
Shipping	1. Testing different shipping options and pricing, 2. Implementing estimated delivery timeframes
Order Confirmation	A/B testing order confirmation page design and layout
Post-Purchase	1. Testing personalized order follow-up emails, 2. Implementing upsell and cross-sell strategies

Key Tips for CRO Success

Setting Clear Conversion Goals

Clearly defined conversion goals are fundamental to CRO success. By aligning conversion goals with your business objectives, you can establish measurable targets for each stage of the conversion funnel. Whether it is increasing sign-ups, driving sales, or improving customer retention, setting clear conversion goals allows you to focus your CRO experiments on specific outcomes and track progress effectively.

Generating Hypotheses for CRO Experiments

Effective CRO experiments are built on solid hypotheses. Conducting research, analysing user feedback, and gathering insights from analytics data are crucial steps in generating meaningful hypotheses. By brainstorming and prioritizing hypotheses based on their potential impact and feasibility, you can ensure that your CRO experiments are targeted and aligned with your conversion goals.

Choosing the Right CRO Experiments

There are various types of CRO experiments, including A/B tests, multivariate tests, and split tests. Choosing the right experiment type depends on the specific objectives and resources of your business. A/B tests are ideal for testing small variations, while multivariate tests allow simultaneous testing of multiple variations. By selecting experiments based on their potential impact and feasibility, you can optimize your conversion funnel effectively.

Implementing CRO Experiments

Implementing CRO experiments involves creating control and variation versions of the elements you want to test. Allocating traffic and running experiments in a controlled and randomized manner ensures accurate data collection. It is crucial to monitor and track experiment progress to identify any issues or anomalies that may affect the validity of the results.

Analysing CRO Experiment Results

Collecting and organizing data from CRO experiments is essential for meaningful analysis. Statistical analysis and significance testing help determine the impact and validity of the variations tested. By interpreting the results and understanding statistical significance, you can draw actionable insights and make data-driven decisions to optimize your conversion funnel.

Tools for CRO

- **Optimizely:** Optimizely is a powerful experimentation platform that enables you to create and run A/B tests, multivariate tests, and personalization campaigns.

- **VWO (Visual Website Optimizer):** It provides an intuitive visual editor for making changes to your website without coding.

- **Hotjar:** Hotjar is a user behaviour analytics and feedback tool that helps you understand how visitors interact with your website. It offers heatmaps, session recordings, surveys, and feedback polls to gather insights and identify areas for improvement.

- **Crazy Egg:** Crazy Egg is another tool that provides heatmaps, scrollmaps, and click reports to visualize user behaviour.

- **AB Tasty:** AB Tasty is a comprehensive CRO platform that offers A/B testing, personalization, and user engagement features.

- **Adobe Target:** Adobe Target is part of the Adobe Experience Cloud and provides powerful testing and personalization capabilities. It enables you to run A/B tests, multivariate tests, and automated personalization campaigns.

- **Convert.com:** Convert.com is a versatile CRO tool that offers A/B testing, multivariate testing, and personalization features.

- **Optimizely X:** Optimizely X is the enterprise-level offering of Optimizely, which provides advanced testing and personalization capabilities.

- **Kameleoon:** Kameleoon is an AI-driven personalization and experimentation platform that offers A/B testing, targeting, and personalization features.

Try different tools and pick the one that suits your needs the most.

PART 2: GENERALIST

Chapter 11

Lean and Agile:

The Dynamic Duo of Growth Marketing

In the world of growth marketing, it is essential to adopt methodologies that promote efficiency, flexibility, and continuous improvement.

Two powerful frameworks that have gained significant recognition and proven their effectiveness are Lean and Agile.

While they have distinct principles and approaches, Lean and Agile complement each other in driving growth and delivering exceptional results.

In this chapter, we will explore how Lean and Agile methodologies work hand in hand to optimize the marketing process and ensure customer-centricity.

We will dive into the core concepts of both frameworks, highlighting their unique contributions and examining how they synergistically enhance the growth marketing journey.

Lean methodology emphasizes eliminating waste, streamlining processes, and maximizing value for customers. It focuses on improving the overall marketing system by identifying and eliminating inefficiencies, bottlenecks, and unnecessary activities.

With Lean, we can uncover opportunities to reduce costs, increase productivity, and deliver better experiences to our target audience.

On the other hand, Agile methodology places a strong emphasis on adaptability, collaboration, and iterative delivery. It empowers marketers to respond swiftly to changing market dynamics, customer feedback, and emerging trends.

Agile enables us to test ideas, gather real-time data, and make informed decisions based on empirical evidence. By embracing agility, we can minimize uncertainty, accelerate time-to-market, and continuously refine our marketing strategies.

While Lean and Agile have their distinct areas of focus, they share a common goal: driving growth through a customer-centric approach.

Lean helps us optimize the marketing process itself, ensuring efficiency and effectiveness in our campaigns. Agile complements Lean by actively involving the end-users, enabling rapid experimentation, and fostering innovation.

Please note that while Lean and Agile methodologies have distinct characteristics, they are often applied in combination to achieve optimal results in growth marketing.

Here is an explanation of both these methodologies based on various factors:

	Lean Methodology	Agile Methodology
Focus	Improving the overall marketing system	Iterative and adaptive delivery
Key Principles	Eliminating waste, streamlining processes	Adaptability, collaboration, and rapid experimentation
Approach	Systematic, process-driven	Agile, flexible, and customer-centric
Benefits	Increased efficiency, cost reduction, value maximization	Faster time-to-market, responsiveness, innovation
Application	Process optimization, waste reduction	Rapid experimentation, iterative improvement
Customer Involvement	Indirect, focusing on system efficiency	Direct, incorporating customer feedback and needs
Decision-making	Data-driven, empirical evidence	Iterative, based on real-time feedback and insights

Use Cases	Streamlining marketing campaigns, reducing bottlenecks	Testing new ideas, adapting to market changes
Collaboration	Team collaboration for process improvement	Cross-functional collaboration for agile execution
Long-term Impact	Sustainable process improvement, continuous growth	Iterative optimization, adaptability to market trends

Building the Lean Mindset

Systems Thinking

Adopt a system thinking approach by considering the interconnectedness of various elements in your growth marketing processes. Look for opportunities to streamline workflows, remove bottlenecks, and optimize the entire system.

Waste Elimination

Identify and eliminate any activities, processes, or resources that do not add value to your customers or contribute to your overall growth objectives. Continuously assess and optimize your marketing efforts to ensure efficiency and effectiveness.

Data-Driven Decision Making

Embrace a data-driven approach to drive your marketing decisions. Collect and analyse relevant data to gain insights into customer behaviour, campaign performance, and market trends. Use this information to inform your strategies and make informed decisions.

Building the Agile Mindset

Iterative Approach

Embrace an iterative mindset by breaking down your marketing initiatives into smaller, manageable cycles. Test, measure, and learn from each iteration, allowing you to make quick adjustments and improvements based on real-time feedback.

Speed and Adaptability

Prioritize speed and adaptability in your marketing execution. Agile marketers understand the importance of being responsive to market changes and customer needs. This allows for faster decision-making and quicker implementation of campaigns and experiments.

Continuous Learning and Improvement

Foster a culture of continuous learning and improvement within your team. Encourage experimentation, gather feedback, and leverage insights to optimize your marketing strategies and tactics. Embrace a growth mindset that values learning from failures and iterating on successes.

Applying Lean and Agile Principles to Growth Marketing

Process Optimization

Use lean principles to identify and eliminate waste in your growth marketing processes. Streamline workflows, automate repetitive tasks, and leverage technology to increase efficiency and reduce unnecessary effort or expenditure.

Experimentation and Testing

Apply agile principles by conducting frequent experiments and tests to validate assumptions, uncover insights, and optimize your marketing strategies. Embrace A/B testing, user feedback, and rapid prototyping to drive data-backed decision-making.

Customer-Centric Approach

Both lean and agile mindsets emphasize the importance of delivering value to customers. Prioritize understanding your target audience's needs, preferences, and pain points. Continuously engage with customers to gather feedback and iterate on your marketing initiatives accordingly.

Cross-Functional Collaboration

Foster collaboration and communication across teams and departments to break down silos and drive synergy. Encourage cross-functional collaboration to leverage diverse perspectives and expertise in developing and executing growth marketing strategies.

By cultivating both the lean and agile mindsets, you can create a culture of continuous improvement, adaptability, and customer-centricity within your growth marketing efforts.

Embrace the systems thinking of lean, while leveraging the speed and flexibility of agile to optimize your processes, deliver value, and drive sustainable growth.

Lean
Reduce waste in
the system

Agile
Deliver to customer
faster

How Lean and Agile Complement Each Other

- While lean focuses on the marketing process, agile also includes the end-user.

- Lean helps us reduce waste within our marketing system, agile helps us reduce uncertainty by testing delivery faster.

- Lean helps us cut costs of the system itself, and with agile, we can avoid costs by avoiding heavy budgets before testing the market.

- You can use lean to reduce waste in a campaign you are already working on for a long time, while you should use agile to try new experiments you have not tested before.

- Lean focuses on improving the system as a whole and agile focuses on letting the target audience decide how the execution should progress.

Those are the key ways in which both principles differ.

Now, since we are growth marketers, we must get our hands dirty to really understand what is happening here!

So, let us consider a real business situation and a growth marketing experiment and apply both lean and agile to this marketing experiment together.

Lean and Agile in A Real Marketing Example

You are a growth marketer. You have got a new client for growth consulting. Your client is a SaaS company that lets their customers invest in big real estate deals by investing very small amounts – like a Kickstarter for real estate.

Here is What You Do

You ideate an experiment where you would build a marketing funnel that will generate traffic via Facebook Ads to a landing page, register the leads to an automated email drip campaign explaining the real estate market and how micro-investing can get big property deals to anyone including college students, and then you will call them to sell them your investment plan.

How to Apply 'Agile' to this Real Marketing Situation

You realize while you can set up the landing page pretty quickly by using a proven template that has worked for you before, but creating the 7-email drip sequence might take a long time.

So, you decide to set up the ads and landing page, and the first 2 emailers of the sequence and test run it with a small budget of $10 on Facebook. Now, you will have data from 100 people if they really click through and sign up and open your first 2 emails.

And as they sign up, you can even start adding the next emails to your sequence before they get to the 2nd one as now, you will have already tested the offer by delivering it to your audience faster.

Congratulations – You just applied agile principles to your growth marketing successfully. And you can do this for all your growth marketing experiments. I take the example of Ad funnels as most of you will understand it easily.

You can also start to see how agile in software development works and how we apply it to marketing in the above example.

How to Apply 'Lean' to this Real Marketing Situation

Your agile marketing experiment was a success! You are now getting a lot of leads from the email drip and your sales team is calling the leads. Like any sales funnel, a few people are interested in your offer out of all the calls, and this is what a funnel should be like.

However, your sales team is also your account management team and now, they have less time to call the actual customers. This means you add a few more people to the team to increase the call volume.

But wait! Then, you meet Mr. Lean!

So, you "think lean" and come up with a better solution: You apply the soft sell and the hard sell within the email drip sequence That is already going out to the leads. And you keep only the final follow up conversation for the call.

Since the audience is already engaged with your funnel, you set up rules to send the sales pitch to those you have opened your emails to, you sit back and relax!

Congratulations – You just applied lean to eliminate waste, save resources, and cut costs in this campaign (system).

So that is how you really apply agile and lean to your marketing and how both principles differ and complement each other so well.

Chapter 12

Introduction to the Growth Funnel

A funnel, just like the name suggests, represents the typical stages a user goes through in the customer journey.

It is a way of **visualizing the process** that turns leads into customers and beyond. Not every user has to go through each stage in a marketer's funnel but it is a great **reference** for the marketer to understand the possibilities of their customer's journey – in order to get the most value from the user as well as to add the most value to the users based on the stage, they are in.

In this chapter, we will build the growth funnel together.

I coined the term A3R3 funnel and I will share the same process that I used to build this funnel.

Before we start, let us look at why we need this funnel.

Why do we need to Build a Funnel Map?

The growth funnel plays a crucial role in driving business growth by providing a structured framework to guide marketing and sales efforts.

It enables businesses to strategically attract, engage, and convert potential customers into loyal advocates.

Here are several reasons why the growth funnel is essential in driving business growth:

Visualizing the Customer Journey:

The growth funnel visually represents the stages a customer goes through from the initial awareness of a product or service to becoming a loyal customer.

It provides a clear roadmap for businesses to understand and optimize each stage of the customer journey.

Identifying Conversion Bottlenecks:

By tracking metrics and analysing data at each stage of the funnel, businesses can identify potential bottlenecks or areas where customers are dropping off.

This allows them to pinpoint weaknesses in their marketing and sales processes and take targeted actions to improve conversion rates.

Targeting Marketing Efforts:

The growth funnel helps businesses focus their marketing efforts on specific stages of the customer journey.

It enables them to tailor their messaging, channels, and tactics to effectively reach and engage customers at each stage.

This targeted approach maximizes the impact of marketing initiatives and increases the likelihood of conversion.

Optimizing Conversion Rates:

The growth funnel provides a framework for testing and optimizing conversion rates at each stage. By experimenting with different strategies, messaging, and user experiences, businesses can continuously refine their approach and increase conversion rates.

This optimization leads to more efficient marketing spend and higher return on investment (ROI).

Driving Customer Lifetime Value:

The growth funnel extends beyond the initial acquisition stage and includes retention and referral stages. By focusing on customer retention and nurturing relationships with existing customers, businesses can increase customer lifetime value (CLV).

Satisfied and loyal customers are more likely to make repeat purchases, provide referrals, and become brand advocates, driving sustainable business growth.

Aligning Marketing and Sales Efforts:

The growth funnel fosters collaboration and alignment between marketing and sales teams. It provides a common framework and shared understanding of the customer journey, enabling both teams to work together seamlessly to drive conversions and revenue.

Data-Driven Decision Making:

The growth funnel relies on data and metrics to track progress, measure performance, and inform decision-making. By leveraging data analytics and insights, businesses can make informed decisions about resource allocation, budgeting, and campaign optimization.

This data-driven approach eliminates guesswork and ensures that growth strategies are based on real-time information.

The growth funnel is instrumental in driving business growth by providing a structured framework for the customer journey.

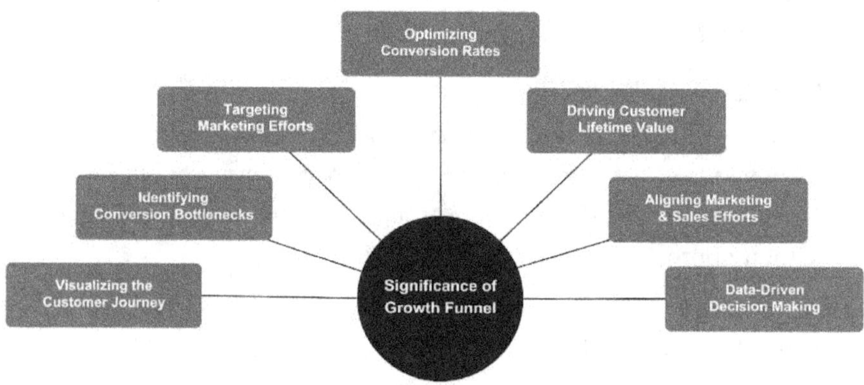

Now, let us use an example and visualize the funnel together.

Building the Growth Funnel

Let us take a simple example where a customer goes through the following stages for startup A:

EXAMPLE 1:

- Step 1: They come across a press release about Startup A.
- Step 2: They visit the website and sign up for the startup's newsletter.

- Step 3: They get an email and take a free demo by the startup.

These 3 steps would sound very familiar but the same can happen in multiple other ways.

EXAMPLE 2:

- Step 1: The user finds a shared social media post mentioning Startup A.
- Step 2: They visit the startup's social media channel and subscribe to their updates.
- Step 3: They find a post giving a free demo and they sign up for it.

Now, both these examples are different however the user is going through the same stages of the customer's journey.

So, what we can do is to name these stages so further instances of such user behaviour can be referenced easily by the marketing team.

Let us call the 3 steps above (in both examples) by easy to reference names:

- Stage 1: Awareness
- Stage 2: Acquisition
- Stage 3: Activation

Now, go back to both the above examples again and see the further possibilities:

Back to Example 1:

- Step 1: They come across a press release about Startup A.
- Step 2: They visit the website and sign up for the startup's newsletter.
- Step 3: They get an email and take a free demo by the startup.
- Step 4: They like the free demo and pay for the product or service.
- Step 5: They renew their service after one month.

- Step 6: They ask one of their friends to sign up for the service too.

And In Example 2, let us say the next steps are as follows:

- Step 1: The user finds a shared social media post mentioning Startup A.

- Step 2: They visit the startup's social media channel and subscribe to their updates.

- Step 3: They find a post giving a free demo and they sign up for it.

- Step 4: They like the free demo and pay for the product or service.

- Step 5: They extend their service contract for a year.

- Step 6: They share the service or product on their social media where their friends can sign up for the service too.

See in both the above examples, the 3 new steps are the same stages of the funnel. This will help us extend our funnel to the following 6 stages:

- Stage 1: Awareness
- Stage 2: Acquisition
- Stage 3: Activation
- Stage 4: Revenue
- Stage 5: Retention
- Stage 6: Referral

This gives us our updated stages of the customer's journey. We can create a simple acronym for the same to remember it:

- Stage 1: Awareness (A)
- Stage 2: Acquisition (A)
- Stage 3: Activation (A)
- Stage 4: Revenue (R)
- Stage 5: Retention (R)
- Stage 6: Referral (R)

That makes it the **AAARRR funnel** or we can shorten it to **A3R3 funnel**. This is a growth funnel any marketer can use.

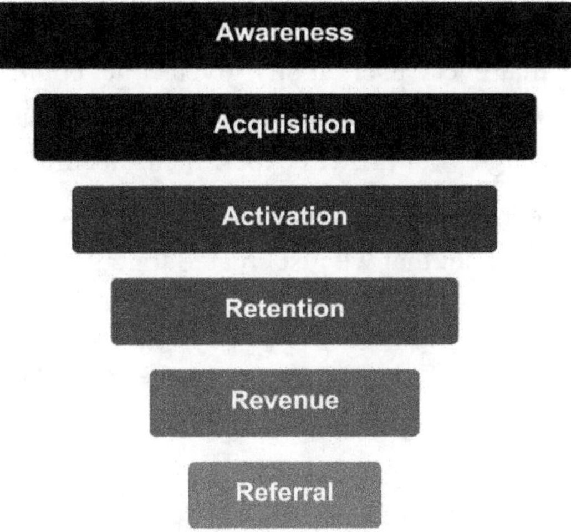

Now, you should be thinking: what about users who churn? What about users who do not refer to their friends? What about user's who, instead of renewing the product or service, go for another product or service by the same startup A?

Well, first of all, you are in the right mindset if you are thinking about all these questions and this would mean you are trying to get into the mind of your users.

The answer to all these questions can be different if we go into the specific scenario of the particular users. However, in general, the answer is that the growth funnel represents the "ideal customer's journey," *not every customer's journey.*

The job of the growth funnel is to act *as a tool* for the marketer to design growth experiments in the potential and ideal stages of the customer's journey.

As you run growth experiments on your customers, you will be able to start creating segments of users who are the best fit for each stage of the funnel. And then, you should focus those growth experiments only on those users.

For example, you will be able to know with the customer's data the set of people who are "most likely to refer to their friends" and design your initial referral marketing experiments to those set of users.

Also, remember that every user, at any given time, could be at any stage of the funnel. The key is to identify sets of users in each stage of the funnel and then design your growth experiments accordingly.

In the next chapter, we will deep dive into the A3R3 funnel or the AAARRR growth funnel that we just created together in this chapter!

Chapter 13

The A3R3 Growth Funnel &

Full Funnel Marketing

In Chapter 12, we went through the process of describing the customer's journey through a growth funnel, which we called the **A3R3 funnel or the AAARRR funnel.**

The funnel describes the stages of an ideal customer's journey – which are the **stages of Awareness, Acquisition, Activation, Revenue, Retention, and Referral.**

In this chapter, we will learn more about the growth funnel and in the chapters following this one, we will be dedicating one chapter to each stage in the funnel.

We saw 2 examples of the user's journey in Chapter 12 where we described how they go through each stage of the funnel.

Now, let us look into the possible methods of driving the entire growth funnel as a growth marketer.

I want you to put your growth marketing hat on. Let us get started.

Let us say Startup A hired you as a growth marketer to define and drive their entire growth marketing funnel. Your first job will be to define the stages of the funnel well and the next step will be to design growth experiments for each stage of the funnel.

Let us say the startup is an edutech company that creates online educational products for 5–15-year-olds.

Here are some of the growth experiments we can plan for this startup:

1. Build influencer partnerships with mom bloggers who have parents of 5 to 10-year-olds as their target audience (since you will be mostly targeting parents of your audience) and create collaborative content with them.

2. Ask the influencers to offer a free trial class by your startup to their audience on an Instagram story.

3. Once parents and their children take the free trial class, offer them an easy onboarding user experiment, free training on the tool you use to teach online.

4. Review the data of how many children took all their paid classes in the package and provide the least likely to renew customers a 20% for their renewal.

5. Provide the first 100 users who have taken a free trial class a 10% discount coupon for their first purchase of any online learning package for their children.

6. Ask the most engaged customers to share your startup's offering with their parents in their community or network.

These are only some of the experiments. I am sure you can think of many more!

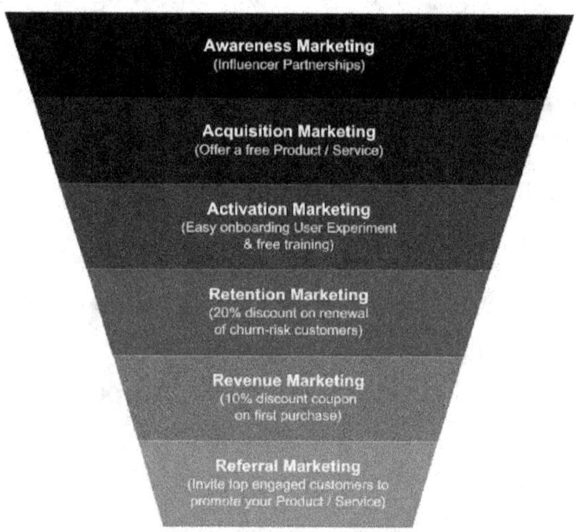

Good job. Now we have one growth experiment idea for each stage of the funnel for this startup.

Let us go back to the examples and give the names of the stages to each experiment:

- Influencer partnerships with mom bloggers – **AWARENESS MARKETING**

- Influencers to offer a free trial class – **ACQUISITION MARKETING**

- Easy onboarding user experiment and free training on the tool – **ACTIVATION MARKETING**
- 20% discount for renewal of churn-risk customers – **RETENTION MARKETING**
- 10% discount coupon for their first purchase of any online learning package – **REVENUE MARKETING**
- Ask the most engaged customers to share your startup's offering – **REFERRAL MARKETING**

This example should give you an idea of how you can design growth experiments for each stage of the funnel.

Here is another example of the A3R3 funnel for an e-learning app:

Funnel Stage	Methods to Drive	Metrics to Measure
Awareness	Content marketing, influencer partnerships, PR	Impressions
Attraction	SEO optimization, social media advertising, webinars	Click-through rate
Acquisition	PPC campaigns, email marketing, referral program	Conversion rate
Activation	Onboarding tutorials, personalized recommendations	User activation rate
Retention	Engagement emails, loyalty programs, community forums	Churn rate
Referral	Referral incentives, social sharing, referral links	Referral conversion rate
Revenue	Upselling, cross-selling, premium features	Average revenue per user

While a user could be in any stage of the funnel at any given time, it is also important to understand that a new startup will have most users in the AAAR stages that are **Awareness, Acquisition, Activation, and Referral**. Throughout this phase of the startup, referral marketing campaigns will be highly ineffective since the referral-ready customer segment will be too small to make a huge difference in the marketing numbers.

This is important to know so you can design and plan your marketing experiments based on what phase your startup is in.

Overview of the A3R3 funnel

Funnel Stage	Methods to Drive	Metrics to Measure	Key Points
Awareness	- Content marketing - SEO (Search Engine Optimization) - SEM (Search Engine Marketing) - Word of Mouth - Influencer collaborations - Drip marketing	- Impressions - Clicks - Traffic - Visitors	- Create valuable and engaging content - Optimize website and content for search engines - Leverage satisfied customers and influencers - Track and analyse campaign effectiveness
Acquisition	- Calls - Direct Messaging (DM) - Webinars - Lead Magnets - Promos - Giveaways	- Traffic - Form Submissions - Lead generation - Conversion rate - Cost per acquisition (CPA)	- Build personal relationships - Offer valuable resources - Run promotions and giveaways - Track acquisition costs and conversion rates
Activation	- Personalization - Gamification - Social proof - Incentives - Education and	- Trial conversion rate - Feature adoption - Engagement	- Provide personalized experiences - Add gamification

		rate	elements
	resources - Support	- Retention rate - Revenue generated - Net Promoter Score (NPS)	- Leverage social proof and incentives - Offer educational resources and support - Measure user engagement and satisfaction
Retention	- Personalized communication - Loyalty programs - Customer support - Upselling and cross-selling - Continuous product improvement	- Customer retention rate - Repeat purchases - Churn rate - Customer Lifetime Value (CLV) - Net Promoter Score (NPS)	- Nurture ongoing engagement and loyalty - Reward and retain existing customers - Provide exceptional customer support - Monitor retention and churn rates - Continuously improve the product and customer experience
Revenue	- Abandoned cart flows - Checkout flows - Relevant product upgrades - Product bundling - Promotions - Freemium model	- Retainers (for services) - Paid conversions from trial users (for SaaS) - Conversion rate - Number of transactions - Average Order Value (AOV)	- Optimize checkout and upsell opportunities - Offer promotions and bundles - Track revenue metrics and customer behaviour

		- Purchases	
Referral	- Referral programs - Affiliate partnerships - Social sharing - Advocate marketing	- Referral conversions - Referral traffic - Conversion rate of referred users - Referral revenue - Advocacy rate - Customer Lifetime Value (CLV) of referred users	- Implement referral programs - Form partnerships with affiliates - Encourage social sharing and advocacy - Measure the impact of referrals on conversions and revenue

When a startup is very mature and has seen multiple cycles of the funnel, all stages of the funnel need to operate in parallel and growth experiments and marketing campaigns always run based on segments across all stages.

Marketing across all the stages of the A3R3 funnel can be referred to as Full Funnel Marketing, which is what Growth Marketing really means.

Full Funnel Marketing

Full stack marketing refers to the practice of utilizing a wide range of marketing tactics and channels to reach and engage with customers at every stage of the marketing funnel. This may include tactics such as SEO, content marketing, social media marketing, email marketing, Influencer marketing, conversion rate optimization, and more.

Who is a Full Stack Marketer?

A full stack marketer is expected to have knowledge of all the different marketing channels and have the ability to use them in a strategic way to achieve the business goals. It also means having the ability to track and measure the effectiveness of marketing efforts and make data-driven decisions to optimize campaigns and improve ROI.

Mastering the AAARRR funnel means being able to effectively execute marketing campaigns that drive growth at each stage of the funnel, from acquiring new users to increasing revenue from existing users.

Many marketers focus on a specific stage of the AAARRR funnel, such as acquisition, and may not have a comprehensive understanding of the entire customer journey. This can lead to a narrow view of the business and limit the effectiveness of its marketing efforts.

On the other hand, a full-stack marketer would have a more holistic view of the business and customer journey, and would be able to understand the interplay between different stages of the pirate metrics.

They would be able to optimize their marketing efforts to not just drive traffic but also increase user engagement, improve retention, and drive revenue. They would also be able to track and analyse the customer journey using pirate metrics and make data-driven decisions accordingly.

In the upcoming chapters, we will deep dive into each stage of the funnel in greater detail, while taking examples from different startups and businesses.

Chapter 14

The Awareness Stage of

the Growth Funnel

In Chapter 13, we discussed the growth funnel which we call the A3R3 funnel or the AAARRR funnel in detail.

We also saw a visual overview of the funnel with the growth marketing experiments you can run for each stage as well as some of the metrics you should measure at each stage of the funnel.

In this chapter, we will deep dive into **the Awareness Stage** of the growth funnel.

The **Awareness Stage** focus on growth activities and experiments that make the potential audience aware in the following situations:

- That a solution exists for a need they have which they may or may not know about

- That a solution is available with our startup

- Educating them as quickly as possible that they have this need and then informing them we can fulfil it

In case they know a specific need they have but they are not "aware" if there is a solution yet, then we must design growth hacking experiments to reach them fast.

Awareness: Scenario 1

Customer is aware or might be aware of their needs.

Here is a step-by-step example experiment in the Awareness Phase of the A3R3 funnel:

- **Step 1:** Go through other close needs the customer may have

- **Step 2:** Make a list of products or tools that solve the closest need

- **Step 3:** Use the audience of these products or tools and market to their audience

Awareness: Scenario 2

Customer is not aware of their own need or requirement (sounds funny but this is often the case)

In this case, we cannot hack awareness of the product or solution directly, but we must first bring out the need and use **Awareness hacks** in parallel for maximum impact.)

Here is a step-by-step example experiment in the Awareness Phase of the A3R3 funnel:

- **Step 1:** Find a podcast or webinar or social media live chat or AMA platform which your target audience subscribes to

- **Step 2:** Share general and specific tips during the event but also use it as a platform to ask questions and help people discover or understand or accept the need

- **Step 3:** Capture their information and use content and retargeting via email or ads to reach them again with your solution for their requirement or need

What You Can Do – Awareness Hacks

- Run validation ad campaigns to their target audience (read more about <u>Validation Marketing</u>, another term coined by Rishabh, which is closely related to the awareness stage of the A3R3 funnel)
- Join their community and have conversations
- Find a few of their users and then leverage word-of-mouth
- Run retargeting campaigns
- Run email marketing drips and newsletters
- Create awareness landing pages with simple opt-ins

What You Should Measure – Awareness Metrics

- Responses to your initiated conversations
- Traffic to your awareness landing page through these experiments
- Impressions on your content and messaging
- Amount of time in terms of minutes of attention to your awareness stage content
- Visits to your website from your Awareness Hacks
- Podcast Impressions and Listen times
- AMA views where you talk about the need or product

This should give you a good starting point to initiate your Awareness Experiments.

You will be able to design your awareness with the above experiments.

However, there are a total of 5 stages of customer awareness that you should make yourself familiar with as a marketer.

5 levels of Awareness

Unaware

At this stage, the customer is unaware of their problem or need and has no knowledge of your brand or product. The goal at this level is to create awareness about the issue and establish a connection with the customer.

Problem Aware

The customer is now aware of their problem or need but is not yet familiar with any potential solutions. The goal at this stage is to educate the customer about the solutions available and introduce your brand as a viable option.

Solution Aware

The customer is aware of the available solutions, including your product or service, but is still unsure about which option is the best fit for their needs. The goal at this level is to differentiate your brand from competitors and showcase the unique benefits and value proposition of your product or service.

Product Aware

The customer is familiar with your product or service and understands its benefits, but they have not yet made a purchase decision. The goal at this stage is to address any remaining objections or concerns, demonstrate social proof, and provide incentives to encourage the customer to make a purchase.

Most Aware

The customer is fully aware of your brand, product, and its benefits, and they may have already made a purchase or are on the verge of doing so. The goal at this level is to maintain a strong relationship with the customer, encourage repeat purchases, and turn them into brand advocates who will refer new customers to your business.

Understanding these different stages of customer awareness is crucial for developing targeted marketing strategies that effectively guide prospects through the buyer's journey and ultimately lead to conversions.

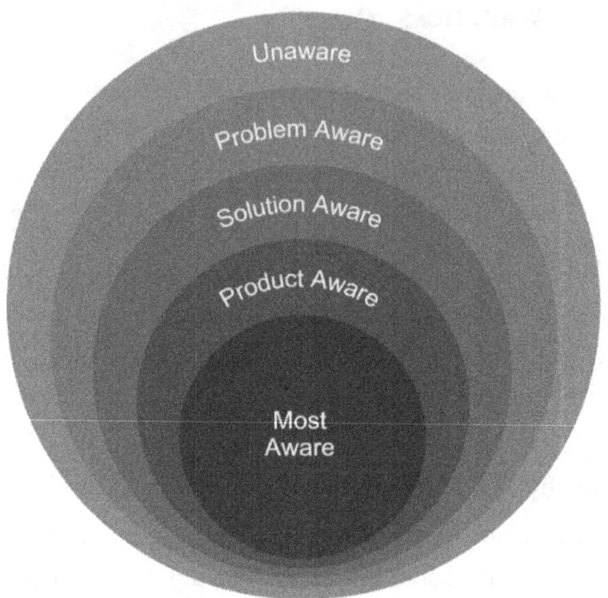

For example, if you decide to run ads for awareness.

You can follow the guidelines below to map the ads to the level of awareness of your target audience:

Stage 1: Unaware

- Ads are typically longer-format and contain copy that leads to a problem.

- They may include questions that help the audience recognize their problem.

- The call-to-action (CTA) is usually simple, such as an invitation to a free workshop or webinar.

Stage 2: Problem Aware

- Ads focus on the problem and build up the desire for a solution.

- The solution is usually mentioned towards the end of the ad.

- The copy emphasizes the pain points and challenges faced by the target audience.

Stage 3: Solution Aware

- Ads mention the solution early on, as it is the primary focus.

- The copy highlights the benefits of the solution but may not mention pricing details yet.

- These ads aim to educate the audience about the solution and its advantages.

Stage 4: Product Aware

- Ads are more specific, mentioning product features, benefits, and pricing.

- They may include comparisons with competitors' products to highlight differentiation.

- Urgency can be leveraged in this stage to encourage the audience to take action.

Stage 5: Most Aware

- Ads are simple and direct, as the audience is already familiar with the brand and product.

- Retargeting ads are often used in this stage, with a minimalistic design and copy.

- The CTA is very direct, focusing on getting the audience to take the final action (e.g., making a purchase).

You can **design multiple awareness experiments** based on the above stages and then plug them into the growth marketing experiments process to start executing and measuring results.

Please note that **AWARENESS MARKETING** should not be confused with finding a Product-Market Fit. Having a product-market fit and the audience having awareness are two different things and should not be confused.

Here, we are talking about startups who have a product-market fit based on their initial **feedback** or MVP iterations.

The problem we are trying to solve here is for them to be able to make their own target audience aware of the product by either first making them aware of the need or by addressing their existing need.

On the other hand, startups or ideas without a product market-kit should go back to the drawing board and focus on finding the fit first and not think about growth hacking or growth marketing.

A product-market fit is the key prerequisite for growth marketing – and should be worked on before diving into any of the core growth marketing funnel experiments.

Strategies for Hacking Brand Awareness

There are several strategies that startups can implement to increase brand awareness. Some of these include:

- **Content Marketing:** Creating and distributing valuable, relevant, and consistent content to attract and engage a clearly defined audience.

- **Influencer Marketing:** Partnering with influencers in your industry to promote your brand to their followers.

- **Public Relations (PR):** Generating positive media coverage and public perception of your brand through press releases, events, and other PR activities.

- **Social Media Marketing:** Utilizing social media platforms to connect with your target audience, share content, and drive engagement.

- **Search Engine Optimization (SEO):** Optimizing your website and content to improve search engine rankings and drive organic traffic.

- **Paid Advertising:** Leveraging paid advertising channels such as Google Ads, Facebook Ads, and display advertising to reach a broader audience.

Startup Examples

Example 1: Dollar Shave Club

Dollar Shave Club, a subscription-based razor and grooming products company, made a splash in the market with its viral video campaign. The company's humorous and engaging video titled "Our Blades Are F***ing Great" garnered millions of views on YouTube and significantly increased brand awareness.

This creative and low-cost marketing tactic not only helped Dollar Shave Club stand out in a competitive market but also attracted a large number of customers to its subscription service.

Example 2: Slack

Slack, the popular team collaboration tool, used a combination of content marketing and PR to build awareness and drive growth.

The company created a series of blog posts and guides that addressed common pain points and challenges faced by teams, positioning Slack as a solution to these problems.

Additionally, Slack leveraged PR to secure media coverage in prominent publications, further increasing brand awareness and credibility.

Example 3: Airbnb

Airbnb, the global home-sharing platform, employed a unique growth hacking strategy to increase awareness and drive user adoption.

The company created a tool that allowed users to cross-post their Airbnb listings on Craigslist, a popular classifieds website.

This tactic not only increased the visibility of Airbnb listings but also attracted a large number of users to the platform, contributing to the company's rapid growth.

Example 4: Canva

Canva, the online graphic design tool, utilized influencer marketing to increase brand awareness and attract users.

The company partnered with prominent bloggers and influencers in the design and marketing space, offering them access to the platform and encouraging them to share their experiences with their followers.

This strategy helped Canva reach a wider audience and establish itself as a go-to design tool for non-designers.

In the next chapter, we will deep dive into the ACQUISITION stage of the growth funnel.

Chapter 15

The Acquisition Stage of the Growth Funnel

In Chapter 14, we explored the Awareness Stage of the AAARRR Growth Funnel in depth.

In this chapter, we will dive deep into the Acquisition Stage.

What is Acquisition?

Acquisition is a significant milestone in your marketing journey where you transition from just measuring numbers on a dashboard to identifying and engaging with real users. It is no longer about anonymous visitors but rather about building connections with potential customers.

At this stage, you have established a way to uniquely identify these users, which opens up new opportunities for retargeting and future engagement. This is where you begin to separate the valuable traffic from the vanity metrics.

To move from Awareness to Acquisition, you need to focus on understanding the traffic that truly matters. It is about identifying the visitors who have displayed genuine interest and can be considered as potential leads or customers. These are users who have taken a specific action or shown clear intent that aligns with your marketing goals.

By acquiring this valuable traffic, you can build a foundation for future marketing efforts and progress further down the conversion funnel. It allows you to establish a connection, nurture relationships, and maximize the value from each interaction.

Remember, the key is not just accumulating numbers, but rather acquiring meaningful interactions that can drive your marketing strategies forward.

Awareness vs Acquisition

So, with this simple definition, you can see the difference between users in the Awareness and the Acquisition stages is just this:

All people who view, visit, click, or see anything about the startup will be considered in the Awareness stage, and of those people, all the ones that can be identified and remarketed to in future will be considered as Acquired or in the Acquisition stage of the funnel.

Metrics for Acquisition

Based on this definition, we can now list some of the metrics in the Acquisition stage and compare them to the Awareness stage that we learned in the last chapter for better understanding:

AWARENESS:

- Clicks
- Reach
- Impressions
- Visitors
- Traffic

ACQUISITION:

- Enquiries
- Subscribers
- Downloads using Lead Forms
- Email Captures
- Phone Number Captures
- Incoming Calls
- Chat Box Captures
- Pixelated Traffic

You can see that "Traffic" falls into Awareness but "Pixelated Traffic" falls into Acquisition since it can be re-targeted through various marketing channels.

Growth Marketing Experiments for the Acquisition Phase

Just by looking at the metrics above, you will know the type of experiments that we can run for the Acquisition stage of the funnel. Here are some examples:

- Setting up online chatbots on the website
- Integrating Facebook Messenger on the website
- Conducting live webinars
- Providing lead magnet downloads
- Promoting free courses for lead generation
- Providing free case study downloads on your website resources
- Giving free trials for your product
- Letting users subscribe to your newsletter

Strategies for Acquisition

There are several strategies that startups can implement to acquire new customers. Some of these include:

- **Landing Page Optimization:** Designing and optimizing high-converting landing pages to capture leads and drive conversions.

- **Email Marketing:** Utilizing targeted email campaigns to nurture leads, promote special offers, and convert prospects into customers.

- **Referral Marketing:** Encouraging existing customers to refer friends and family in exchange for incentives, such as discounts or free products.

- **Paid Advertising:** Leveraging paid advertising channels, such as Google Ads, Facebook Ads, and display advertising, to target and acquire new customers.

- **Social Media Marketing:** Engaging with your target audience on social media platforms and promoting your products or services to drive conversions.

- **Content Marketing:** Creating and distributing valuable, relevant, and consistent content to attract, engage, and convert your target audience.

Startup Examples

Example 1: PayPal

PayPal achieved market penetration in the highly competitive online payment market through a paid referral strategy.

However, another significant growth hack they used was partnering with eBay, which helped them acquire a large user base and establish themselves as a trusted payment method.

Example 2: Uber

Uber, the ride-sharing platform, leveraged a combination of referral marketing and promotional offers to acquire new customers.

The company provided promo codes to existing users, which they could share with friends and family. When a new user signed up using the promo code, both the referrer and the new user received a discount on their next ride.

This strategy helped Uber expand its customer base rapidly and establish a strong presence in the market.

Example 3: HubSpot

HubSpot, the inbound marketing and sales software, utilized content marketing to acquire new customers.

The company created valuable resources, such as blog posts, eBooks, webinars, and templates, to attract and engage its target audience.

By offering these resources for free, HubSpot was able to capture leads, nurture them through email marketing, and ultimately convert them into customers.

Example 4: Casper

Casper, the online mattress retailer, used a combination of social media marketing and influencer partnerships to acquire new customers.

The company engaged with its target audience on social media platforms, sharing user-generated content and promoting its products.

Additionally, Casper partnered with influencers and celebrities, who shared their positive experiences with the brand, further driving customer acquisition.

Example 5: Mint

Mint, a personal finance management app, utilized content marketing to acquire new customers. The company created a blog that provided valuable financial advice and tips, attracting a large audience, and establishing Mint as a credible source of financial information. This content-driven strategy helped Mint grow its user base and led to its eventual acquisition by Intuit.

Example 6: Buffer

Buffer, a social media scheduling tool, used guest posting as a growth hack to acquire new users.

The company's founder, Joel Gascoigne, wrote guest posts for popular blogs in the marketing and social media space, providing valuable content and introducing Buffer to a wider audience. This strategy helped Buffer gain traction and acquire new customers.

Example 7: Canva

Canva, the online graphic design tool, utilized influencer marketing to increase brand awareness and attract users. The company partnered with prominent bloggers and influencers in the design and marketing space, offering them access to the platform and encouraging them to share their experiences with their followers.

This strategy helped Canva reach a wider audience and establish itself as a go-to design tool for non-designers.

Example 8: Grasshopper

Grasshopper, a virtual phone system provider, launched an unconventional marketing campaign called the "Chocolate-Covered Grasshopper".

The company sent out 5,000 chocolate-covered grasshoppers to influential people, along with a personalized note and a link to a video about their service. The campaign generated significant buzz and helped Grasshopper acquire new customers.

Example 9: Airbnb

Airbnb, the home-sharing platform, used a growth hacking technique by piggybacking on Craigslist.

The company allowed users to cross-post their listings on Craigslist, which helped Airbnb tap into Craigslist's large user base and acquire new customers.

This unconventional approach played a significant role in Airbnb's rapid growth.

Example 10: Tinder

Tinder, the popular dating app, focused on college campuses to acquire new users. The company's founders visited college campuses and organized parties where attendees were required to download the app to enter.

This grass-roots marketing approach helped Tinder establish a strong presence among college students and acquire a large user base.

Example 11: HelloFresh

HelloFresh, a meal-kit delivery service, used street marketing to acquire customers. The company set up stands in high-traffic areas, offering free samples of their meals and distributing discount vouchers.

This face-to-face approach helped HelloFresh create a buzz and acquire new customers in a highly competitive market.

Example 12: BarkBox

BarkBox, a subscription box service for dog owners, partnered with animal shelters and rescue organizations. The company donated a portion of their proceeds to these organizations and encouraged them to promote BarkBox to their supporters. This cause-driven marketing approach not only helped BarkBox acquire new customers but also generated positive PR and brand loyalty.

All the above examples help drive the Acquisition Phase of the Growth Funnel. These are just for reference. You should design growth experiments based on the product or service you are driving growth for.

Chapter 16

The Activation Stage of the Growth Funnel

In this chapter, we will focus on the next stage, which is Activation.

What is Activation?

Activation is the next big step in your growth funnel.

In this stage, you are having the first interaction with your product or service.

This is where the user has gone from being a user on your website or just a lead to interacting with your product and thus upgrading to being a prospect.

This interaction with your product or service can be in the form of demo signup, sign up for a free/basic account, or even a sales response in some cases.

All of these can be actions to look for to tag a user in the activation stage.

Think of activation as the first date in a relationship – it is the foundation for What is to come. The type of interaction can vary depending on your business, but it typically involves some sort of initial sign-up or registration.

Once a user is in the activation stage, they are more invested in your product and more likely to continue using it.

This is why it is essential to optimize the activation process and make it as seamless and frictionless as possible for your users.

Activation vs Acquisition

Remember that in Chapter 15, we explored the concept of Acquisition, which is the stage where you can identify a user and witness the transition from mere "traffic" to an actual "user".

In the corresponding sales terminology, a user in the Acquisition stage can be best called a lead while a user in the Activation stage can actually be called a prospect.

This is why Activation is closer to the Revenue stage of the funnel as leads narrow down to prospects which would further narrow down to paying clients (we see this in the next stage of the funnel).

Note: *This is why I place Revenue right after Activation and not at the bottom of the funnel, like the old Pirate metrics, that were made around Freemium apps.*

Metrics for Activation

Here are the key metrics for the activation stage of the funnel:

- Product Demo Signups
- Free Trial Signups
- Free Account Signup
- Sales Demo Signup

These are some of the metrics that show Activation.

Examples of Activation

Some of the examples that mark the Activation stage include:

- When a user completes their first ride with Uber, experiencing the convenience and reliability of the service firsthand.

- When a company creates its free plan on Slack, indicating their commitment to improving communication and collaboration within their organization.

- When a new Gmail account user sends their first email, embracing the power of digital communication and becoming an active participant in the online world.

- When a customer receives a grocery delivery from Instacart, enjoying the convenience of having their essentials delivered right to their doorstep for the first time.

- When a customer books a free audit call or report from a service provider, demonstrating their interest and engagement with the provider's expertise and potential solutions.

Strategies for Activation

There are several strategies that startups can implement to activate new customers. Some of these include:

- **Onboarding:** A seamless onboarding process can help new users understand and navigate your product or service more efficiently. Consider offering step-by-step tutorials, helpful tips, and guides to ensure that your users have a positive experience from the start.

- **Personalization:** Incorporating personalized elements into your product or service can help users feel more connected to your brand. Collect user data to understand their preferences and behaviours, and then use that data to tailor the user experience to their unique needs.

- **Gamification:** Adding game-like elements, such as challenges, badges, and rewards, can boost user engagement and motivation. Gamification can make your product or service more enjoyable and entertaining, encouraging new users to explore and engage more deeply.

- **Incentives:** Offering incentives, such as discounts, free trials, or exclusive content, can be an effective way to encourage new users to take action and engage with your product or service. These incentives can help to build trust and foster a positive relationship with users from the outset.

- **Customer Support:** Exceptional customer support can go a long way in building trust with new users. Make sure that your support team is knowledgeable, responsive, and helpful in addressing user concerns and resolving issues quickly and effectively. This can help to create a positive user experience and encourage users to stay engaged with your product or service.

Startup Examples

Example 1: Slack

Slack, the team collaboration platform, used a combination of onboarding and gamification to activate new users.

When a user first signs up for Slack, they are guided through a series of onboarding steps that introduce them to the platform's features and functionalities.

Additionally, Slack incorporates gamification elements, such as progress bars and achievement badges, to motivate users to complete tasks and engage with the platform.

Example 2: Duolingo

Duolingo, the language learning app, leverages gamification and personalization to activate new users.

The app uses game-like elements, such as points, levels, and streaks, to motivate users to complete lessons and practice regularly.

Duolingo also personalizes the learning experience by adapting the content and difficulty based on individual user performance.

Example 3: Evernote

Evernote, the note-taking and organization app, activates new users by offering a seamless onboarding process and providing incentives.

Upon signing up, users are guided through a series of onboarding steps that introduce them to Evernote's features and functionalities.

The app also offers a free trial of its premium version, encouraging users to explore and utilize its advanced features.

Example 4: Spotify

Spotify, the music streaming service, activates new users through personalization and incentives.

The platform creates personalized playlists based on users' listening habits and preferences, ensuring a tailored and engaging experience.

Spotify also offers a free trial of its premium service, allowing users to explore the ad-free and offline listening features before committing to a subscription.

Example 5: Headspace

Headspace, the meditation and mindfulness app, activates new users through a combination of onboarding, personalization, and incentives.

Upon signing up, users are guided through a series of onboarding steps that introduce them to the app's features and meditation techniques. Headspace also personalizes the user experience by offering tailored meditation plans based on individual goals and preferences.

Additionally, the app provides a free trial of its premium subscription, allowing users to access a wide range of meditation sessions and features before committing to a paid plan.

Activation is the stage where your user realized your product's promise or value proposition. Hence, this stage can better predict revenue.

It also shows how well and efficiently you spent money on the last stage of Acquisition.

Your "activated" users are much more likely to be retained and generate revenue for your startup or business. This leads us to the next stage which can be either Revenue or Retention depending on what kind of business you are in.

The order of the Retention and Revenue stages in the A3R3 Growth Funnel can vary depending on the type of business and its specific goals.

In some cases, focusing on Revenue before Retention may be more appropriate, while in others, prioritizing Retention before Revenue might be the better approach.

For example, a subscription-based business, such as a streaming service like Netflix, might prioritize Retention first, as retaining customers and keeping them engaged with the platform is crucial for generating recurring revenue. The same is the case with social media apps like Twitter or Facebook.

On the other hand, a business with a one-time purchase model, such as an e-commerce store selling high-ticket items, might emphasize Revenue first, as the primary goal is to drive sales and maximize the value of each customer transaction.

In this case, retention efforts, such as customer loyalty programs and personalized marketing, can be implemented after the initial purchase to encourage repeat business and increase customer lifetime value.

The order of the Retention and Revenue stages should be determined by the unique characteristics and objectives of the business, ensuring that the growth funnel is aligned with the company's overall strategy and goals.

In this book, we will discuss Retention next but remember that for a business, they can always be in a different order as explained above.

Chapter 17

The Retention Stage of the Growth Marketing Funnel

In this chapter, we will focus on the next stage, which is Retention.

Retention is the process of keeping customers engaged with your product or service and maintaining long-term relationships with them.

It is a critical aspect of the growth funnel, as retaining customers can lead to increased revenue, and customer lifetime value, and eventually also drive word-of-mouth referrals.

The Retention Stage

Retention is the next crucial stage of focus in the AAARRR funnel after the initial purchase or activation. At this point, your customers are looking for the transformation that your product or service has promised to offer.

It is your chance to deliver on that promise and maintain their loyalty for the long-term.

The key to retention is ensuring customer satisfaction and providing value that is equivalent to the consumer's investment.

By doing so, you create a more engaging user experience, reducing the likelihood of churn and maximizing the customer's lifetime value.

As a growth marketing campaign, retention metrics take centre stage, allowing you to measure the effectiveness of retention strategies.

The focus is on keeping the customer engaged, informed, and satisfied through relevant content, personalized offers, and exceptional customer service.

With the right retention strategies, you can improve user satisfaction and increase loyalty to cultivate a strong customer base.

Successful retention is not just about retaining the customer, but building a relationship that fosters loyalty, advocacy and can lead to repeat purchases, higher order values and reduce your marketing acquisition cost in the long-term.

Metrics to Measure Retention

Customers can say "yes" to your business at multiple touch points after the initial transaction. All metrics that can measure this "yes" are retention-related metrics. Some examples are:

Contract Renewal Rate

This metric measures the percentage of customers who choose to renew their contracts or subscriptions at the end of a contract period. A high contract renewal rate indicates that customers are satisfied with the product or service and are willing to continue using it.

Customer Lifetime Value (CLV)

CLV is the total revenue a business can expect from a single customer over the entire duration of their relationship. It is an important metric for understanding the long-term value of a customer and helps businesses make informed decisions about customer acquisition and retention strategies.

Churn Rate

Churn rate is the percentage of customers who stop using a product or service within a specific time period, typically expressed on a monthly or annual basis. A high churn rate indicates that customers are not satisfied with the product or service, and retaining customers is a challenge for the business.

Monthly Recurring Revenue (MRR) Churn

MRR churn is the amount of monthly recurring revenue lost due to customer cancellations or downgrades in a given month. This metric helps businesses understand the impact of churn on their monthly revenue and identify areas for improvement in their retention strategies.

Gross Revenue Retention (GRR)

GRR measures the percentage of revenue retained from existing customers over a specific time period, without considering any new customer revenue. This metric helps businesses understand how well they are retaining revenue from their existing customer base and can be used to identify potential issues with customer satisfaction or product quality.

% Returning Customers

This metric calculates the percentage of customers who make repeat purchases or continue to use a product or service over time. A high percentage of returning customers indicates strong customer loyalty and satisfaction with the product or service.

Net Promoter Score (NPS)

NPS is a customer satisfaction metric that measures the likelihood of customers recommending a product or service to others. It is calculated by asking customers to rate their likelihood of recommending the product or service on a scale of 0-10, with 10 being the most likely. Customers are then categorized as promoters (9-10), passives (7-8), or detractors (0-6). NPS is calculated by subtracting the percentage of detractors from the percentage of promoters.

% Revenue from Existing Customers

This metric measures the percentage of total revenue generated by existing customers, as opposed to new customers. A high percentage of revenue from existing customers indicates strong customer retention and loyalty, while a low percentage may indicate a need to improve customer satisfaction and retention strategies.

Customer Stickiness

Customer stickiness refers to the likelihood of customers continuing to use a product or service over time, even in the presence of competitors or alternative solutions. Stickiness can be measured using metrics such as churn rate, contract renewal rate, and customer lifetime value. A high level of customer stickiness indicates strong customer loyalty and satisfaction with the product or service.

Retention campaigns focus on improving one or more of these metrics.

Most subscription-focused startups measure retention in terms of churn rate, which is basically the rate at which customers stop doing business with you.

Churn leads to lost revenue, and That is what churn rate measures – at what rate you are losing potential revenue. It is the opposite of the growth rate.

Similarly, most ecommerce startups measure % revenue from repeat customers or % of orders from repeat customers along with Lifetime Customer Value.

There is another metric, 'TBP,' i.e., time between purchases that is usually measured by ecommerce startups alongside the % revenue from repeat customers.

As with all stages of the funnel, when you design any campaign in the retention stage, make sure to start by deciding your focus metric for the campaign.

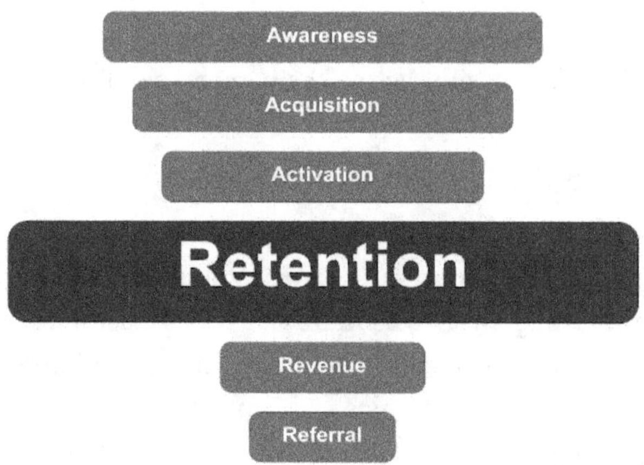

Strategies for Hacking Retention

There are several strategies that startups can implement to retain customers and build long-lasting relationships. Some of these include:

- **Customer Feedback:** Regularly collecting and acting on customer feedback to improve your product or service and address any issues or concerns.

- **Personalization:** Tailoring the customer experience to individual preferences, behaviours, and needs to create a more engaging and satisfying experience.

- **Customer Support:** Providing exceptional customer support to address user concerns, answer questions, and resolve issues quickly and effectively.

- **Loyalty Programs:** Implement loyalty programs that reward customers for their continued business and engagement, encouraging them to remain loyal to your brand.

- **Re-Engagement Campaigns:** Running targeted re-engagement campaigns to rekindle interest and bring back inactive or lapsed customers.

Startup Examples

Example 1: Amazon Prime

Amazon Prime, the subscription service by Amazon, effectively retains customers by offering a wide range of benefits and perks, such as free shipping, access to streaming content, and exclusive discounts.

By continuously adding value to the Prime membership, Amazon encourages customers to remain loyal and engaged with the platform.

Example 2: Starbucks

Starbucks, the global coffee chain, retains customers through its Starbucks Rewards loyalty program.

The program allows customers to earn stars for every purchase, which can be redeemed for free drinks, food, and other rewards.

By offering personalized incentives and a seamless mobile app experience, Starbucks encourages customers to keep coming back and remain loyal to the brand.

Example 3: Buffer

Buffer, the social media management tool, retains customers by providing exceptional customer support and continuously improving its product based on user feedback.

The company is known for its responsive and helpful customer support team, which addresses user concerns and resolves issues quickly.

Additionally, Buffer actively solicits feedback from its users and implements improvements to enhance the overall user experience.

Example 4: Fitbit

Fitbit, the wearable fitness tracker company, retains customers by offering personalized insights, challenges, and social features that encourage users to stay engaged with the platform.

Users can track their progress, set goals, and compete with friends, which keeps them motivated and engaged with the Fitbit ecosystem.

Example 5: Peloton

Peloton, the home fitness equipment, and streaming workout platform, retains customers by offering a wide variety of engaging and interactive workout classes, as well as fostering a strong community.

Users can access live and on-demand classes, track their progress, and compete with friends on the leaderboard.

The platform also offers community features, such as social media integration and virtual workout groups, which help users stay motivated and connected with fellow fitness enthusiasts.

Chapter 18

The Revenue Stage of the Growth Funnel

When the Pirate metrics was first introduced, Revenue was placed at the very bottom of the funnel after Acquisition, Activation, Retention, and Referral.

But in my version of the AAARRR growth metrics, I place Revenue right after Activation.

Many startups and marketers find it more relevant to prioritize revenue generation earlier in the funnel to ensure profitable growth. In fact, for some businesses, revenue generation may even precede customer retention. Therefore, it is beneficial to tweak and customize the AAARRR growth metrics in a way that fits the specific business model and its objectives.

In this book, we have discussed the retention stage before revenue. But depending on the type of business, revenue generation may take precedence over customer retention.

What is the Revenue Stage?

It is all about the money.

Revenue is the income generated from the sale of goods or services, and it is a critical component of a startup's growth and success.

To drive sustainable growth, startups need to develop effective revenue models and strategies that align with their target customers' needs and preferences.

Ask the question: How many users start paying for your product or service? It is important to think about revenue in terms of both the number of users who pay for your product as well as the actual revenue (in amount) that you can bring in.

Based on different business models, what you are measuring will be slightly different.

If you are running a recurring subscription business, and a customer has paid for an annual plan, you are going to assume that revenue amount from the customer for the next one year.

Using the amount here, we can calculate our Potential Order Value and compare it with our CAC.

You can also predict LTV using prediction models at this stage, but I would warn against that for new startups and businesses.

Revenue Metrics and Examples

Here are some examples of the Revenue stage from different types of businesses:

- **B2B Services:** One example of a revenue-generating action in the B2B services industry is when a customer signs an annual contract. This signifies a commitment to utilizing the company's services for a specified duration.

- **Freemium Products:** In the case of freemium products, a customer paying for a premium version indicates a revenue milestone. This action demonstrates that the customer sees value in the product and is willing to invest in additional features or functionality.

- **Paid Product Plans:** Another revenue stage example is when a customer purchases any paid plan of a product. This could include different tiers or levels of service that provide enhanced benefits or customization options.

- **E-Commerce Websites:** When a customer places an order on an eCommerce website, it represents a key revenue action. This could involve the purchase of physical products, digital goods, or services offered on the platform.

These revenue-generating actions play a significant role in the success of businesses across various industries. By tracking and analysing these actions, companies can gain insights into their revenue streams and make informed decisions to drive growth and profitability.

Strategies for Hacking Revenue

There are several strategies that startups can implement to generate revenue and drive growth. Some of these include:

- **Freemium Model:** Offering a free version of your product or service with limited features while charging for premium features or additional resources. This model allows users to try your product before committing to a paid plan, increasing the likelihood of converting them into paying customers.

- **Subscription Model:** Charging customers a recurring fee to access your product or service. This model provides predictable and consistent revenue, making it easier to plan for growth and allocate resources.

- **Transactional Model:** Charging customers a one-time fee for your product or service, typically based on usage or consumption. This model can be effective for products with a high perceived value and low frequency of use.

- **Advertising Model:** Generating revenue through advertising on your platform, such as display ads, sponsored content, or affiliate marketing. This model can be effective for platforms with a large user base and high engagement.

- **Tiered Pricing:** Offering multiple pricing plans or packages with varying features and benefits, allowing customers to choose the option that best meets their needs and budget. This strategy can help maximize revenue by catering to different customer segments and price sensitivities.

- **Cross-selling:** Offer complementary products or services that align with customers' existing purchases, encouraging them to buy more from your startup.

- **Upselling:** Encourage customers to upgrade to a higher-priced plan or product with more features or benefits, increasing their overall spending.

- **Bundling:** Combine multiple products or services into a single package at a discounted price, incentivizing customers to purchase more at once.

- **Subscription Model:** Offer a subscription-based pricing model to ensure consistent revenue and retain customers for longer periods.

Startup Examples

Example 1: Amazon

Amazon, the e-commerce giant, employs a transactional model to generate revenue through the sale of products on its platform.

Amazon charges sellers' fees based on the sale of goods and services, allowing the company to generate revenue from a vast range of products and services.

Amazon also uses various pricing hacks to improve customer revenue.

Here are five of them:

1. **Dynamic Pricing:** Amazon adjusts its prices frequently based on factors such as demand, competition, and customer behaviour. This strategy helps Amazon stay competitive and maximize revenue by offering the right price at the right time.

2. **Price Anchoring:** Amazon uses price anchoring to influence customer behaviour by listing a high-priced item alongside a lower-priced item, making the lower-priced option seem like a better deal.

3. **Competitive Pricing:** Amazon focuses on competitively pricing popular products to create a perception of being the cheapest destination for customers. This strategy attracts customers and encourages them to make purchases.

4. **Psychological Pricing:** Amazon employs psychological pricing techniques, such as setting prices just below whole numbers (e.g., $9.99 instead of $10) to make products appear more affordable and increase sales [3].

5. **Promotions and Discounts:** Amazon offers various promotions and discounts to attract customers and encourage them to buy more products, increasing overall revenue.

Example 2: Byjus

BYJU'S, an Indian edtech company, has implemented various strategies to improve its Average Order Value (AOV) and Lifetime Value (LTV).

Here are some ways BYJU'S has achieved this:

1. **Product Bundling:** BYJU'S offers bundled courses and learning materials that cater to different age groups and subjects. By providing comprehensive packages, they encourage customers to purchase higher-value bundles, which increases the AOV.

2. **Personalized Learning Plans:** BYJU's uses data-driven insights to create personalized learning plans for students, increasing the perceived value of their offerings and driving higher AOV and LTV.

3. **Subscription Model:** BYJU'S offers subscription-based pricing for its courses, ensuring consistent revenue and higher LTV by retaining customers for longer periods.

4. **Cross-selling and Upselling:** BYJU'S leverages its vast product portfolio to cross-sell and upsell additional courses and materials to existing customers, increasing both AOV and LTV.

Example 3: Starbucks

Starbucks implements various strategies to improve customer lifetime value (LTV). Here are five ways the company achieves this:

1. **Loyalty Program:** Starbucks has a popular loyalty program called Starbucks Rewards, which offers customers points for every purchase. These points can be redeemed for free drinks and food, motivating customers to spend more and stay engaged with the brand

2. **Personalization:** Starbucks uses customer data to provide personalized offers, recommendations, and experiences. This increases the perceived value of their offerings and encourages customers to make additional purchases

3. **Customer Satisfaction:** Starbucks focuses on customer satisfaction by providing high-quality products and services. Bain & Co found that a 5% increase in customer satisfaction can increase LTV by 25% to 95%

4. **Mobile App:** Starbucks' mobile app allows customers to order ahead, pay, and earn rewards, making the customer experience more convenient and seamless. This drives customer engagement and increases LTV

5. **Seasonal Offerings:** Starbucks frequently introduces limited-time seasonal offerings, such as the Pumpkin Spice Latte, which creates a sense of urgency and exclusivity, encouraging customers to make additional purchases

Chapter 19

The Referral Stage of the Growth Marketing Funnel

Happy customers become brand advocates and spread the word. This "word of mouth" marketing is explored in the Referral stage of the marketing funnel.

The Referral Stage

This is often the most overlooked and underappreciated stage of the AAARRR funnel.

This is where your existing customers refer your product or service to their friends and family, and the rest of their own network.

Referrals are a form of word-of-mouth marketing, which is one of the most trusted and effective ways to acquire new customers.

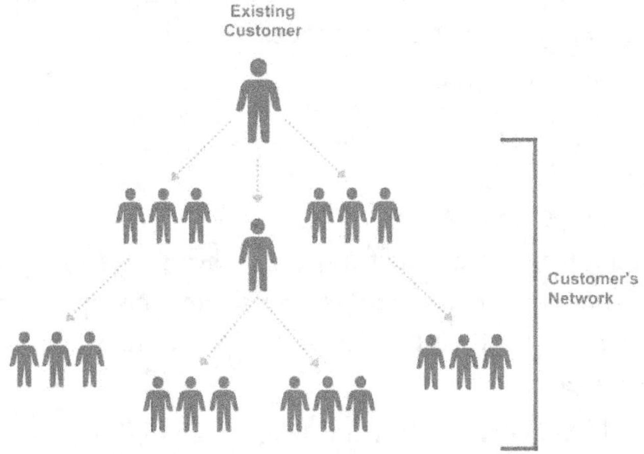

According to Nielsen, 92% of consumers trust recommendations from friends and family over any other form of advertising

"Every day startups" really started talking about the Referral stage of the funnel after some big successes came from the likes of Dropbox's "invite friends and earn more storage" campaign that led to 3900% growth within 15 months and later, Uber's 'refer and earn free rides for both you and your friend' campaign.

There are some key data points and rationale that show the effectiveness of referrals:

- Referred deals are usually closed faster than deals sourced from other channels

- The lifetime value of referred customers is usually higher than non-referral clients

- Most people trust recommendations from people they know compared to ads

Organic content channels such as email and social media and often used to run referral campaigns alongside in-app and in-platform promotions.

Metrics to Measure Referrals

Referral marketing metrics are best defined as specific to the campaign you are planning to run. However, there are some key metrics that can help you measure your overall referral effectiveness.

Some of the referral metrics are:

- Number of active users sharing invites
- Referral link CTRs
- Invitees per referrer

It is also important to track metrics from other stages of the marketing funnel separately for the referred user segment. This helps compare the customer behaviour of customers that come from referrals vs. non-referred customers.

Since referral campaigns will again lead to Acquisition, Revenue, and Retention (and potentially more referrals), you can track metrics in those stages again for the referred customer segment.

For example:

- Churn rate of referred customers
- Retention rate of referred customers

- The lifetime value of referred customers

The key idea here is to segment your referred customers and measure their behaviour vs non-referred customers.

You can also create multiple referred customer cohorts within the segment to track customers referred during different times.

The Viral Coefficient

As referral programs grow, you will hopefully notice the "viral" addition of customers as a result. "Viral" is anything that is created through spreading across from one to many.

The viral coefficient measures how well your referrals are converting.

It takes into account both the number of referrals as well as the conversion rate.

Viral Coefficient is calculated as follows:

Viral Coefficient = (# invitations sent per customer) X (% conversion rate of the invitations)

This can give you an outlook on how well you can acquire viral growth through referral campaigns.

It is also important to consider the Viral Cycle Time along with the Viral Coefficient to get a complete picture of HOW WELL and HOW FAST your startup or business can grow using referral marketing.

Incentives for Referral Campaigns with Startup Examples

Some of the incentives you can offer for referral campaigns are as follows:

- **Cash Rewards:** Offer cash rewards for successful referrals.

  For example, PayPal's referral program provided cash rewards to both the referrer and the referred when they signed up and completed a qualifying transaction.

- **Discounts:** Provide discounts on future purchases for successful referrals.

  For example, Uber offers ride discounts to both the referrer and the referred when the referred user completes their first ride using a referral code.

- **Free Products or Services:** Offer free products or services for successful referrals.

  For example, Dropbox, for instance, provides additional free storage space to both the referrer and the referred when the referred user signs up for a new account.

- **Gift Cards:** Give gift cards for successful referrals.

  Airbnb offers travel credit in the form of gift cards to both the referrer and the referred when the referred user completes their first stay or experience.

- **Exclusive Access:** Grant exclusive access to premium features, content, or events for successful referrals.

  For example, Robinhood offers a free stock to both the referrer and the referred when the referred user signs up and links their bank account.

- **Charitable Donations:** Make a donation to a charity on behalf of the referrer for each successful referral.

Toms Shoes, for example, donates a pair of shoes to a child in need for every successful referral.

- **Loyalty Points:** Award loyalty points for successful referrals, which can be redeemed for discounts, products, or services.

  The Marriott Bonvoy program offers loyalty points to both the referrer and the referred when the referred user completes a qualifying stay.

- **Subscription Extensions:** Extend the subscription period for successful referrals.

  For example, Grammarly offers a free one-week premium subscription extension to both the referrer and the referred for each successful referral.

- **Swag Or Branded Merchandise:** Provide branded merchandise, such as t-shirts, hats, or stickers, for successful referrals.

  For example, InVision offers branded merchandise to both the referrer and the referred when the referred user signs up for a new account.

- **Tiered Rewards:** Offer tiered rewards based on the number of successful referrals, encouraging customers to refer more people.

  For example, Tesla's referral program offers increasing rewards, such as charging credits and exclusive event invitations, based on the number of successful referrals made by a customer.

By offering a variety of incentives, you can motivate your customers to participate in your referral campaign and help drive growth for your business.

Referral Marketing Case Studies

Dropbox

Dropbox, a cloud-based file storage and sharing service, is a prime example of a startup that successfully leveraged referral marketing to drive growth. In its early days, Dropbox implemented a referral program that rewarded both the referrer and the referred with additional free storage space (up to a certain limit) when the referred user signed up for a new account.

This incentive was highly relevant to its users, as it directly addressed their need for more storage space.

As a result, Dropbox's referral program led to a 60% increase in signups, with referrals accounting for 35% of its daily signups at the peak of the program. This referral marketing strategy played a significant role in Dropbox's rapid growth and its current user base of over 600 million users.

Airbnb

Airbnb, a platform for booking accommodations and experiences, has successfully used referral marketing to expand its user base and increase bookings.

In 2011, Airbnb launched a referral program that offered travel credit to both the referrer and the referred when the referred user completed their first stay or experience. The program was designed to encourage existing users to invite their friends and family to try Airbnb, capitalizing on the trust built through personal connections.

By 2015, Airbnb's referral program had resulted in over 900,000 new members and more than 2 million nights booked.

The success of Airbnb's referral program is attributed to its attractive incentives, seamless referral process, and effective promotion through email and social media channels.

Uber

Uber, the ride-hailing service, has also benefited from a successful referral marketing strategy. Uber's referral program offers ride discounts to both the referrer and the referred when the referred user completes their first ride using a referral code.

This program incentivizes existing users to share their referral code with friends and family, while also providing an incentive for new users to try the service.

Uber's referral program has played a significant role in its rapid global expansion and growth, with referrals contributing to more than 30% of its daily sign ups at one point.

By offering relevant incentives and making the referral process simple, Uber has been able to leverage word-of-mouth marketing to drive growth and increase its user base.

Revolut

Revolut, a digital banking and financial services platform, has effectively utilized referral marketing to grow its user base.

Revolut's referral program offers cash rewards to both the referrer and the referred when the referred user signs up and completes a qualifying transaction. This incentive encourages existing users to share their referral code with friends and family, while also providing an incentive for new users to try the platform. Revolut's referral program has contributed significantly to its growth, with the company now boasting over 15 million users.

By offering relevant incentives and making the referral process simple, Revolut has been able to leverage word-of-mouth marketing to drive growth and increase its user

Evernote

Evernote, a note-taking and organization app, has effectively used referral marketing to expand its user base and increase premium subscriptions. Evernote's referral program offers points to both the referrer and the referred when the referred user signs up for a new account.

These points can be redeemed for various rewards, such as premium subscription extensions or increased storage capacity. The program is designed to encourage existing users to invite their friends and family to try Evernote, capitalizing on the trust built through personal connections. Evernote's referral program has contributed significantly to its growth, with the company now boasting over 250 million users.

The success of Evernote's referral program is attributed to its attractive incentives, seamless referral process, and effective promotion through various channels.

These referral marketing case studies demonstrate the power of referral programs in driving growth for startups.

Chapter 20
Lean Analytics

Lean Analytics is a data-driven approach that focuses on using metrics and iterative experimentation to drive startup growth and innovation.

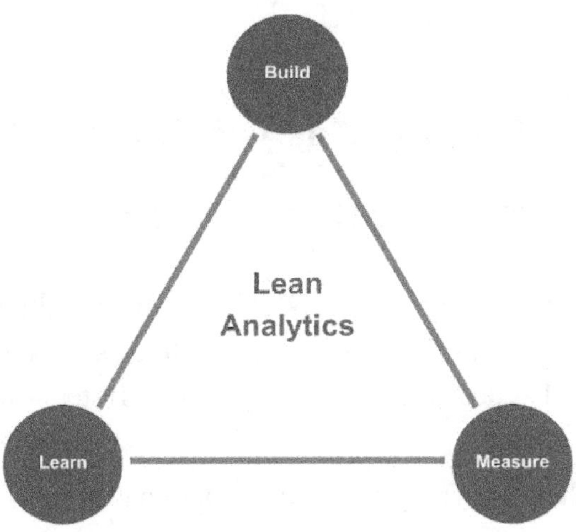

Key Principles of Lean Analytics

1. **Build-Measure-Learn:** Emphasizes the importance of rapid experimentation, measurement, and learning from data to make informed decisions.

2. **Small Batches:** Encourages breaking down initiatives into small, manageable increments to gain quick feedback and iterate accordingly.

3. **Validated Learning:** Prioritizes validating assumptions and hypotheses through data analysis and customer feedback to reduce risk and increase chances of success.

4. **Actionable Metrics:** Advocates for measuring metrics that provide actionable insights and align with business objectives.

5. **Pivot or Persevere:** Encourages being open to changing direction based on insights gained from data analysis and customer feedback.

As you can see based on the above principles, lean analytics works really well for startups that are always iterating and moving fast.

However, it is also beneficial applied to all sizes of businesses to reduce waste and improve constantly.

Benefits of Using Lean Analytics Methodologies

Here are some benefits of using the lean analytics principles for your business:

- **Rapid Feedback Loop:** Lean Analytics allows startups to quickly test assumptions, gather feedback, and make data-informed decisions, leading to faster iterations and improvements.

- **Cost Efficiency:** By focusing on actionable metrics and iterative experimentation, startups can optimize their resource allocation, minimizing wasted efforts and expenses.

- **Customer-Centric Approach:** Lean Analytics puts the customer at the center by continuously seeking feedback, validating hypotheses, and aligning products and services with customer needs.

- **Agility and Adaptability:** Startups and businesses can easily adapt to market changes and pivot their strategies based on insights gained from Lean Analytics, increasing their chances of success.

Now, let us look at how Lean Analytics methods can be applied to different stages of the A3R3 funnel.

Integration of Lean Analytics with the A3R3 Funnel

Awareness Stage

- **Lean Analytics Methods:** Utilizing digital marketing analytics, social media monitoring, and market research to track brand awareness metrics such as website traffic, social media reach, and search engine visibility.

- **Metric Example:** Brand impressions, measured through website visits, social media followers, and impressions.

Acquisition Stage

- **Lean Analytics Methods:** Implementing conversion rate optimization techniques, A/B testing, and funnel analysis to optimize user acquisition channels and improve conversion rates.

- **Metric Example:** Conversion rate, measured by the percentage of website visitors who become registered users or customers.

Activation Stage

- **Lean Analytics Methods:** Analysing user onboarding and activation processes, conducting user behaviour analysis, and using cohort analysis to understand user engagement and activation patterns.

- **Metric Example:** Activation rate, measured by the percentage of registered users who complete key actions or reach a predefined level of engagement.

Revenue Stage

- **Lean Analytics Methods:** Implementing pricing experiments, analysing revenue streams, and utilizing customer lifetime value (CLV) analysis to optimize monetization strategies.

- **Metric Example:** Average revenue per user (ARPU), calculated by dividing total revenue by the number of active users or customers.

Retention Stage

- **Lean Analytics Methods:** Monitoring user retention metrics, analysing user feedback, and conducting churn analysis to identify factors affecting user retention and develop retention strategies.

- **Metric Example:** User retention rate, measured by the percentage of active users or customers who continue to use the product or service over a specific period.

Referral Stage

- **Lean Analytics Methods:** Tracking referral programs, analysing viral coefficient, and using net promoter score (NPS) to measure customer satisfaction and referral potential.

- **Metric Example:** Referral rate, measured by the percentage of users or customers who refer the product or service to others.

Next, let us look at some of the lean analytics methods as applied to real startups.

Lean Analytics Methods with Startup Examples

Lean Analytics Method	Startup Example
Cohort Analysis	Airbnb: Analysing cohorts of hosts to understand host retention rates and improve host onboarding processes.
A/B Testing	Dropbox: Conducting A/B tests on different pricing plans and features to optimize conversion rates and user engagement.
Funnel Analysis	Slack: Analysing the user journey from signup to active usage to identify areas of drop-off and improve user onboarding.
MVP (Minimum Viable Product)	Buffer: Launching a minimal version of the social media scheduling tool to validate market demand and gather user feedback.

Customer Surveys and Interviews	SurveyMonkey: Conducting surveys and interviews to gather insights on user preferences and needs, and improve survey creation and analysis tools.
Net Promoter Score (NPS)	Tesla: Measuring customer satisfaction and loyalty through NPS surveys to understand drivers of customer advocacy and improve overall customer experience.
Viral Coefficient Analysis	WhatsApp: Tracking how many new users each existing user invites to the platform, measuring the viral growth and network effects.
User Behaviour Analytics	Spotify: Analysing user interactions and listening patterns to personalize recommendations and enhance the user experience.
Lifetime Value (LTV) Analysis	Amazon: Calculating the lifetime value of customers based on their purchase history to optimize marketing strategies and customer retention efforts.
Social Media Monitoring	Airbnb: Monitoring social media channels to track user feedback, identify trends, and manage brand reputation and customer satisfaction.

These examples highlight how real startups have applied Lean Analytics methods to drive growth, improve user experience, and make data-driven decisions.

Common Challenges and How to Overcome Them

Challenge 1

- Limited resources for data collection and analysis - Startups often face resource constraints when it comes to collecting and analysing data.

- To overcome this, they can prioritize the collection of essential data points and leverage cost-effective analytics tools and platforms.

Challenge 2

- Data overload and analysis paralysis - With vast amounts of data available, startups can struggle with analysis paralysis.

- It is crucial to identify the most relevant metrics and focus on actionable insights that directly impact business objectives.

Challenge 3

- Resistance to change and organizational buy-in - Implementing Lean Analytics may require cultural and organizational shifts.

- Startups should foster a data-driven culture, educate stakeholders about the benefits, and demonstrate tangible results to gain buy-in and overcome resistance.

This can be harder for big corporations. And working with multiple Fortune 500 companies as a consultant myself, I was able to myself see their own transformation from being hesitant to adopting lean analytics methods for their business units.

Lean Analytics Tools

You can use various tools to implement Lean Analytics methods for your startup or business.

Here are some tools I personally use and recommend:

- **Google Analytics:** A powerful web analytics tool that provides valuable insights into website traffic, user behaviour, and conversion rates. It can be used for funnel analysis, cohort analysis, and tracking key metrics.

- **Mixpanel:** A user analytics platform that helps track user interactions and behaviour within a web or mobile application. It enables A/B testing, funnel analysis, and user segmentation.

- **Optimizely:** A popular A/B testing tool that allows you to experiment with different variations of your website or app to optimize conversion rates and user experience.

- **Hotjar:** A tool that provides heatmaps, visitor recordings, and conversion funnels to visualize user behaviour and identify areas for improvement on your website or app.

- **Qualtrics:** A comprehensive survey tool that allows you to collect user feedback, conduct customer satisfaction surveys, and gather insights for decision-making.

- **Kissmetrics:** An analytics platform focused on customer behaviour and conversion tracking. It helps measure and optimize key metrics throughout the customer journey.

- **Amplitude:** A product analytics tool that provides behavioural analytics, user segmentation, and funnel analysis to gain insights into user engagement and retention.

- **Crazy Egg:** A tool that generates heatmaps and click-tracking reports to visualize user interactions and optimize website design and user experience.

- **SEMrush:** A versatile tool for competitive analysis, keyword research, and SEO optimization. It can help identify market trends, track organic rankings, and evaluate marketing performance.

- **Buffer:** A social media management tool that enables scheduling and analysing posts across various platforms. It can be used to track social media engagement, audience growth, and conversion rates.

These tools provide startups with the necessary capabilities to implement Lean Analytics methodologies, track relevant metrics, and gain actionable insights to make data-driven decisions and drive growth.

The choice of tools depends on the specific needs and goals, and the methods from the lean analytics framework you are using.

PART 3: SPECIALIST

Chapter 21

Copywriting & Content Hacks

As attention spans are shrinking, the key is to write persuasive copy and engage the user, one statement at a time.

This chapter explores the art of crafting effective copy and leveraging content hacks to boost growth.

The best place to start is to use copywriting frameworks. This will help you not just get started with your copywriting, but also start at the right place.

Let us explore these frameworks:

Copywriting Frameworks

The AIDA Framework

AIDA stands for Attention, Interest, Desire, Action:

Getting the user's Attention, generating Interest, building Desire, and ultimately leading them to take action.

Let us break it down and provide examples of how each stage can be employed in marketing copy:

Attention

The first step is to grab the reader's attention and make them stop scrolling or ignore distractions.

This can be achieved through compelling headlines, eye-catching visuals, or intriguing opening statements.

- On YouTube, for example, this will be the title and thumbnail of the video.
- On LinkedIn, it will be the hook which is the opening statement.

- On email, it will be your subject line, and the first line of the email (for those who open)

Here are some examples:

- "Discover the Secret to Flawless Skin in 7 Days." (Timeline)
- "Are You Tired of Wasting Money on Inefficient Workout Equipment?" (Question)
- "Unlock the Secrets to Financial Freedom before you turn 30." (Number/Timeline)
- "How to make $10,000 with online businesses?" (Number/Currency)

Interest

Once you have captured their attention, it is essential to build interest by providing valuable information or addressing a pain point.

This is where you highlight the unique selling points or benefits of your product or service.

Examples include:

- "Our cutting-edge skincare formula is scientifically proven to reduce wrinkles by 30%." (Adding data)
- "Our revolutionary exercise machine guarantees visible results in just 15 minutes a day." (Low time commitment)

Desire

After building interest, it is time to create a strong desire for your product or service.

This can be done by showcasing testimonials, success stories, or by emphasizing the emotional benefits.

Examples include:

- "Join thousands of satisfied customers who have transformed their skin and regained their confidence."
- "Imagine how incredible you'll feel when you achieve your fitness goals and become the envy of your peers."

Imagine waking up to a spotless, clutter-free home every day.

Action

The final stage is to prompt the reader to take action.

This can be a call-to-action (CTA) that urges them to make a purchase, sign up for a newsletter, or make contact.

Examples include:

- "Limited time offer: Buy now and receive a 20% discount!"

- "Do not miss out! Subscribe to our newsletter to get 10% on your first purchase."

- "Get a personalized quote within 5 minutes."

As you can see in the examples above, specifying the timeline or numbers or amounts helps.

This makes the copy more persuasive.

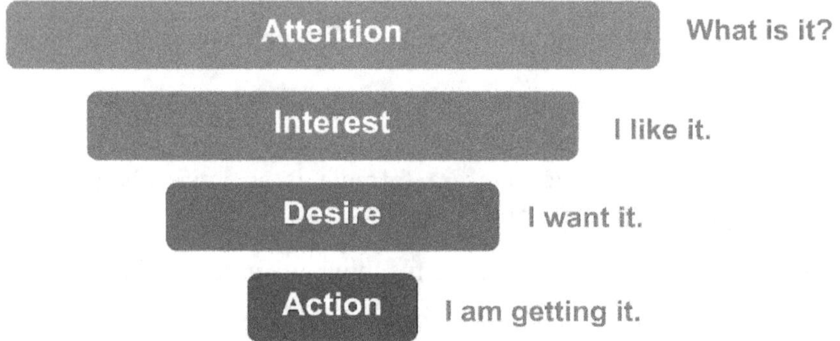

The BAB Framework

This framework consists of three stages:

1. **Before:** In this stage, you paint a picture of your audience's current situation or pain point. Describe the challenges or frustrations they may be experiencing, and you help them connect with their problem emotionally.

2. **After:** This stage focuses on the ideal outcome or result that your audience desires. You help them imagine what their life could be if they solved their problem and got the result they wanted.

3. **Bridge:** This stage connects the Before and After by explaining how your product or service can help them reach their desired result. Highlight the unique features and benefits of your offering and explain how it can solve their problem.

This can be easily spotted in the fitness industry in the following general theme:

- **Before:** "Struggling to lose weight and get in shape no matter how much you exercise or how healthy you eat?"

- **After:** "Imagine waking up every morning to see a healthier and happier version of yourself in the mirror. Our fitness program can help you lose weight, gain confidence, and feel great about yourself."

- **Bridge:** "Our program combines proper nutrition, personalized plans, and expert guidance, so you can enjoy your fitness journey and achieve long-lasting results. Join us now and start getting in shape on your own terms!"

However, it is used by almost every industry.

It is just harder to spot in some industries than others.

Here is another example:

- **Before:** "Tired of spending hours on manual data entry every day, dealing with errors and inconsistencies that impact your business's efficiency?"

- **After:** "Imagine saving up to 50 hours a month, with a 30% decrease in errors, leading to a more streamlined and profitable business."

- **Bridge:** "Our automated data management software uses artificial intelligence and machine learning to help you optimize your data entry process and improve accuracy. Sign up for our free trial now."

Now, let us get into the startup space.

Here are some of the key BAB messages from startups which you will now be able to spot on their landing pages, ad copy, email copy, and across other channels as well:

Dropbox

- **Before:** Are you tired of having your files saved across different devices locally and worrying about losing your important files?

- **After:** Imagine having all your files securely stored in the cloud, accessible from any device, and automatically synced across all your devices.

- **Bridge:** With Dropbox, you can store, share, and access your files from anywhere, making file management effortless and worry-free.

Airbnb

- **Before:** Planning a vacation, can be stressful and expensive, with limited options for accommodation.

- **After:** Imagine staying in unique and affordable homes, connecting with locals, and experiencing a city like a local.

- **Bridge:** With Airbnb, you can book a wide range of accommodations, from cozy apartments to luxurious villas, and immerse yourself in the local culture wherever you go.

Slack

- **Before:** Email overload and scattered communication tools can hinder productivity and collaboration.

- **After:** Picture a streamlined workspace where teams can communicate, share files, and stay organized in one place.

- **Bridge:** With Slack, you can centralize your team's communication, integrate with essential apps, and boost productivity with efficient collaboration.

Canva

- **Before:** Designing graphics and visuals can be time-consuming and require specialized skills.

- **After:** Imagine creating professional-looking designs with ease, even if you have no design experience.

- **Bridge:** With Canva, you gain access to a user-friendly design platform with a vast library of templates, fonts, and graphics to bring your creative ideas to life.

If you look at the above examples, you will notice that the BAB framework is also great for planning the transformation you want to provide as your startup to your user.

Using AI to Generate Copy and Content

AI tools can significantly streamline content creation processes.

While AI tools can generate content, they still require human guidance and creativity.

Marketers can use AI-generated content as a starting point and personalize it to suit their brand voice and tone.

I personally use a framework called the 3Ps framework to write copy with AI.

The 3Ps of AI Copy Generation

1. Prepping: Data preparation and training the AI model

Before utilizing AI tools, marketers need to prepare data, clean, and organize it, and train the AI model to understand their specific brand and target audience.

For instance, a marketing team might collect data from customer interactions, social media engagements, and website interactions.

This data can include customer feedback, purchase history, and preferences.

Let us take an example of an e-commerce startup that wants to use AI to generate product descriptions.

The marketing team gathers data on customer behaviour, such as which products are most popular, frequently searched keywords, and customer reviews.

They also analyse competitor product descriptions to understand market trends and effective language.

These inputs can then be provided to the AI tool being used.

2. Prompting: Providing the right inputs and instructions to the AI tool

This is where you actually prompt.

Most people do this first and skip the prepping which leads to a generic output.

Clear and concise instructions ensure that AI-generated content aligns with the brand's messaging and meets the marketing objectives.

Specify the tone and style, ensuring consistency with their brand voice.

3. Personalization: Customizing and fine-tuning AI-generated content

Adding a personal touch to AI-generated content is essential to ensure that it resonates with the brand's identity and connects with the audience on a deeper level.

I personally add a lot of examples from my clients.

This helps get an output which is human-like, and fits my own personal tone of voice and style of writing.

Adding examples from my own experience also helps add personalization to the content.

Growth Hacks Using Content

You can use content in different stages to drive growth.

Let us look at different growth hacks that leverage content, for each stage of the funnel:

Certainly! Here are three content hacks for each stage of the A3R3 funnel:

Awareness Stage

- **Guest Blogging:** Collaborate with industry influencers or popular blogs to write guest posts that showcase your expertise and provide value to their audience. This helps you reach a broader audience and establish your brand as an authority in the field.

- **Social Media Contests:** Organize engaging contests on social media platforms to encourage user participation and increase brand visibility. Offer attractive prizes related to your product or service to attract more participants and create a buzz around your brand.

- **Infographics and Visual Content:** Create eye-catching infographics and visual content that highlight interesting statistics or insights related to your industry. Share them on social media and relevant platforms to capture the attention of your target audience.

Acquisition Stage

- **Content Lead Magnets:** Offer valuable lead magnets, such as e-books, whitepapers, or exclusive guides, in exchange for visitors' email addresses. This tactic helps you build a qualified email list and nurture potential customers through targeted email campaigns.

- **Webinars and Online Workshops:** Host webinars or online workshops that address common pain points of your target audience. Use them as opportunities to demonstrate your product or service's value and provide real-time solutions to their problems.

- **Interactive Quizzes and Assessments:** Create interactive quizzes or assessments that engage users and offer personalized results based on their answers. This not only provides valuable insights to users but also helps you gather data to tailor your marketing approach.

Activation Stage

- **Onboarding Videos:** Develop onboarding videos that guide new users through the key features and functionalities of your product or service. This helps users understand your offering better and increases their chances of becoming active users.

- **Email Drip Campaigns:** Set up email drip campaigns with personalized content to keep users engaged after sign-up. Use triggered emails to send relevant information, tips, and success stories that encourage users to take specific actions.

- **Customer Success Stories:** Share customer success stories and testimonials that highlight the positive outcomes achieved by using your product or service. This social proof helps build trust and confidence in potential customers, nudging them to become active users.

Revenue Stage

- **Limited-time Offers:** Create a sense of urgency by offering limited-time discounts or exclusive deals to encourage potential customers to make a purchase. Highlight the value they can get from acting quickly.

- **Upselling and Cross-selling Content:** Implement upselling and cross-selling strategies by recommending complementary products or premium versions to existing customers through targeted content or emails.

- **Abandoned Cart Emails:** Send personalized abandoned cart emails to remind customers of the items they left behind and offer incentives like free shipping or discounts to persuade them to complete the purchase.

Retention Stage

- **Educational Newsletters:** Send educational newsletters or email series to provide ongoing value to your customers. Share industry insights, best practices, and tips to help them maximize the benefits of your product or service.

- **Loyalty Programs:** Implement a customer loyalty program that rewards repeat purchases or referrals. Offer exclusive perks or discounts to loyal customers to incentivize them to continue engaging with your brand.

- **Feedback and Surveys:** Regularly seek feedback from customers through surveys or feedback forms to understand their needs and pain points better. Use this data to improve your product or service, making it more aligned with customer expectations.

Referral Stage

- **Referral Contests:** Organize referral contests where existing customers can earn rewards or discounts for referring new customers to your business. This incentivizes word-of-mouth marketing and encourages customer advocacy.

- **Shareable Content:** Create shareable content, such as infographics, videos, or entertaining posts, that customers are more likely to share with their network. This amplifies your reach and attracts potential customers through referrals.

- **Referral Landing Pages:** Set up dedicated referral landing pages that explain the benefits of referrals and make it easy for customers to refer their friends or colleagues. Ensure the process is simple and straightforward to encourage participation.

These content hacks align with the various stages of the A3R3 funnel and can help your startup optimize its content strategy to drive growth and achieve business objectives.

As you can see, content plays an important role in each stage of the funnel.

Using the writing frameworks we discussed earlier, leveraging AI, and then applying these hacks across the funnel is how we can use content to drive growth.

The following section of this chapter was contributed by Radhakrishnan KG (RK).

Bio: RK is a seasoned digital marketing strategist and the founder of WebNamaste, dedicated to helping SMBs accelerate their revenue growth. With over a decade of experience, Radhakrishnan has developed a unique approach to content marketing, focusing on nurturing leads and driving conversions. His innovative strategies have consistently delivered impressive results, earning him recognition as a pioneer in the industry.

Types of Content for Nurturing Leads

Here are some types of contents that can be leveraged to nurture leads:

Case Studies

Case studies are real-world examples of how a product or service has benefited others. They are powerful tools for building trust and demonstrating the value of an offer. An example of a case study could be "Doubling Productivity: A Success Story from X Company," which showcases tangible results.

Case studies provide social proof and demonstrate how your product or service can solve real-world problems. They allow potential customers to see themselves in the success stories of others, making your offer more relatable and compelling.

White Papers

White papers are in-depth reports on a specific topic. They are excellent for showcasing expertise and providing valuable information to an audience. A white paper could delve into a topic like "Bridging the Gap: The Integral Connection Between Marketing and Sales," providing a comprehensive look at aligning marketing and sales efforts.

White papers position your brand as a thought leader in your industry, demonstrating your deep understanding of the subject matter and ability to provide solutions.

Exclusive Reports

These are akin to white papers but are often more data-driven. They provide exclusive insights that an audience cannot find anywhere else. A report such as "2023 Key Trends: The Driving Forces of Successful Hybrid Work Culture," based on research from Fortune 500 companies, can offer unique insights.

Exclusive reports not only provide valuable information but also demonstrate your brand's commitment to staying at the forefront of industry trends and data.

Educational Video Series

Videos are a compelling way to engage an audience. An educational video series can provide valuable information and establish authority in a field. A series like "Mastering LinkedIn: A 3-Part Guide to Personal Branding" can share actionable tips and strategies for building a strong personal brand on LinkedIn.

Video content is highly engaging and can simplify complex topics, making them more accessible to your audience.

Email Nurture Sequence

This is a series of emails designed to engage leads, provide value, and gradually guide them toward a purchase. An email sequence such as "The Subscriber Surge: A 7-Day Guide to Growing Your Email List" can share strategies for expanding an email list.

Email nurture sequences allow you to maintain regular contact with your leads, providing them consistent value and gently guiding them down the sales funnel.

Newsletters

Regular newsletters can keep an audience engaged and a brand at the forefront of their minds. A newsletter like "The Insight Dispatch: Monthly Musings from the Foothills of the Himalayas" can share insights, updates, and valuable content related to a specific industry.

Newsletters are a great way to keep your audience informed about your latest offerings, industry trends, and valuable insights.

By leveraging these types of nurture content, leads can be effectively engaged, trust can be built, and they can be guided toward making a purchase. The key to successfully nurture content is to provide value and build a relationship with the audience.

Each piece of content should be strategically designed to move the lead closer to a buying decision, positioning your brand as the best solution to their problem.

Chapter 22

Email Marketing for Growth

Contributing Author: Deepak Kanakaraju

Bio: Deepak Kanakaraju is a digital marketing consultant, author, and mentor.

Deepak is the founder of PixelTrack, a digital marketing agency and training company. He has worked with brands like Nikon, HDFC, and Mercedes Benz guiding them on their digital marketing strategy.

He runs a digital marketing training program called the Micro Internship program for students and has mentored more than 12,000 students in digital marketing. He also runs AlphaClub, a mastermind program for business owners who want to scale their business 10x.

He is an avid reader and a biker. He rides a Kawasaki most of the time. He also believes that Bitcoin will change the world for the better. He lives in Bangalore with his wife Sandhya.

Email marketing is one of the most important components of digital marketing. A lot of people do not understand how to use email marketing. The biggest mistake that most marketers make is to use email marketing as the top-of-the-funnel acquisition mechanism.

While cold emailing can help you get started finding some customers and clients, it is not scalable and unfair to bombard people with offers that they are not looking forward to receiving from you. Buying email databases and bulk-messaging people is not just immoral and unethical but also illegal in many countries.

Permission Marketing via Email

Email marketing works best as a middle-of-the-funnel strategy to warm up your leads. You can nurture your leads over some time by offering good content. Using email to warm up leads is basically "permission" marketing. I learned this from Seth Godin through his book "Permission Marketing". You are getting permission from your leads to market to them.

The best way to grow your email list is by advertising a lead magnet such as an eBook, email course, or mini-video series.

To get people on your list, you need to interrupt people on social media by running ads, but That is the only time you interrupt them.

Once they opt-in for your content series, you send content to them. Your subscribers should look forward to receiving valuable content from you. It is like paying a toll fee to enter a private road once and then not having to pay every mile.

Do not destroy the trust and permission the audience has given you by sending too many promotions to your list. If you abuse the permission you have earned, then the permission will be revoked at a click of a button.

Your leads are taking a leap of faith and "paying" you with their contact details. They "pay" attention to your content and you should give an "ROI" for that attention they pay you. That transaction builds trust which leads to monetary conversions later.

Add subscribers and send content slowly and steadily. For the first 2 weeks, just offer good content and build that trust and anticipation among your audience. After that, you can slowly monetize your list by making offers to your audience.

Email Marketing Tools That Help You

Many email marketing tools in the market help you do permission marketing. You can use Ghost.org to create email newsletters. Or you can get people to opt-in to your drip marketing sequence that is configured on an email marketing tool such as ActiveCampaign or ConvertKit.

Add subscribers to your email list slowly and steadily. Do not add 1000s of subscribers at the same time. Make sure you have double opt-in enabled for your subscription.

Double opt-in means that subscribers have to confirm their email ID before they start receiving emails from you. This reduces bounce rate and spam complaints and helps you deliver your emails to the inbox properly.

Along with email marketing, you can add your audience to an online community where discussions can take place. This will create an affinity towards your brand and make your brand come to life.

You can also do a live webinar once or twice a month to engage with your audience. This will help your audience remember your face and voice.

Whenever your audience gets an email from you, they will read the emails and your voice and your face will play in their mind. This increases the response rate and stickiness of your email campaigns.

An email list becomes your primary distribution channel and the biggest asset in your business. I have built an email list of 500,000 subscribers over the past 5 years and this is a result of generating over 2,000,000 (two million) leads.

Many subscribers will unsubscribe and go cold (they do not open emails for more than 90 days). You must constantly prune your email list and the fans will stick around.

If you want a highly active list of 1,000,000 people on your email list, you might need to generate 10,000,000 (10 million) leads over the course of several years to make sure that you are getting the most involved and engaged 10% on the list. That is one of the best ways to build an audience.

Email Marketing vs Social Media

Email marketing is better than most distribution channels because it gives you a direct connection with your audience with no middlemen.

A lot of people build their following on social media channels such as YouTube, Instagram, and Twitter. But the problem with social media channels is that the users who "follow" you are not your users.

They are the users of the platform. They signed up on the platform using an email ID and phone number. You do not have access to the email IDs of your YouTube subscribers.

If you have 100,000 YouTube subscribers, and if you post a brand-new video on your channel, the YouTube algorithm decides the quality of your content based on several metrics and makes a decision to push it to a percentage of your audience. It is rarely 100%.

I have 122,000 subscribers on my YouTube channel, and if I post a new video and do not do any external promotions, the footage only gets around 2,000 views. That is less than 2% of my subscribers.

If your thumbnail is not shocking enough to get a high CTR and if your headline is not attention-grabbing enough, then you might not be able to reach all your subscribers.

In this case, I am being a slave to the algorithm.

I must do stuff to appeal to the algorithm, which takes away focus on what I want to communicate with my audience.

However, if you are sending an email to all your subscribers, it will reach all of them (if you maintain a good domain and IP reputation).

No one is going to filter or block your messages. Your reach is not going to be dependent on the subject line or the content of your email. You have already earned permission to send them emails.

If they do not like your emails, they will unsubscribe from your emails and then no more emails will be received from them. This permission becomes an asset for your business.

Email marketing helps you understand your audience deeply and design products and services that they need.

Startups fail because they do not get product market fit. When you build an email list, you build your distribution before you build the product.

You are doing market-product fit instead of trying to get the product-market fit. You are getting access to a market first, understanding the needs of your audience and then you can create any product that will fit into the market.

Email Marketing Segmentation and Customization

Unlike social media channels, email marketing also gives you the power to customize your content according to the subscriber that is receiving the content. You can segment your audience and send different content to different segments.

For example, in my email list, I have 3 major types of audiences. Students, Professionals, and Entrepreneurs. I can use tags and segments to put them into different buckets. Certain emails will go to the entire audience, and certain emails will only go to a specific segment.

We have a product called "Career Kickstarter" which is designed for fresh college graduates.

Most students and interns take that course. It would not make sense if I promoted that product to business owners. Business owners need help with setting up a marketing funnel and increasing their revenue. They are not looking to kickstart their careers.

Our digital marketing agency services are for business owners. I can mail only business owners who might be interested in our service because students do not need digital marketing services right now.

Certain email marketing tools also allow you to add conditional content within your emails.

Instead of sending separate emails to different segments, you can use if/else conditions to add content within an email copy and it will be shown only to the people who have certain tags.

It might be difficult for me to show you how and it is beyond the scope of this content, but I want you to realize the possibilities of sending the right message to the right people at the right time which is only possible with email marketing.

Email Marketing is Here to Stay

A lot of people think that email marketing is dead. They think that it will be replaced by Facebook ads messenger or WhatsApp or some other new form of communication channel.

How long have you been using your email ID? 5 years? 10 years? Just like phone numbers will not go away, emails will not go away.

The first email between two computers was sent in 1971. The first website was published in 1991. Email predates websites by 20 years. Email predates social media apps by more than 30 years.

Email marketing is here to stay as long as people use emails and emails are not likely to fade out because of the network effects.

The above content was contributed by Deepak Kanakaraju

Now that we understand the importance of email marketing as Deepak explained to us, let us look at Email marketing's application to the A3R3 funnel and how email can be used across the full funnel.

Email Marketing Across the A3R3 Funnel

Let us look at how email marketing can be used across different stages of the A3R3 funnel, irrespective of the industry:

Awareness

- **Email Newsletter:** Send out informative newsletters sharing industry insights, trends, and valuable content to showcase your expertise.

- **Educational Content:** Share e-books, webinars, and blog posts that address common pain points in your industry.

Acquisition

- **Lead Magnets:** Offer downloadable resources like e-books, guides, or templates in exchange for email subscriptions.

- **Webinar Invitations:** Invite prospects to webinars showcasing your product/service and how it solves their problems.

Activation

- **Onboarding Series:** Send a series of emails introducing new users to your product's features, guiding them through setup, and encouraging engagement.

- **Getting Started Guides:** Share tutorials and tips to help users maximize the value of your product or service.

Revenue

- **Promotions and Discounts:** Send exclusive offers, discounts, or early access to your email subscribers to drive sales.

- **Cross-selling and Upselling:** Recommend related products or premium features based on the user's purchase history.

Retention

- **Engagement Campaigns:** Send personalized content based on user behaviour to maintain their interest and engagement.

- **Re-engagement Campaigns:** Reach out to inactive users with incentives or new features to reignite their interest.

Referral

- **Referral Program:** Encourage subscribers to refer friends in exchange for rewards, sending reminder emails about the program.

- **Shareable Content:** Provide content That is easily shareable, encouraging subscribers to forward emails to their network.

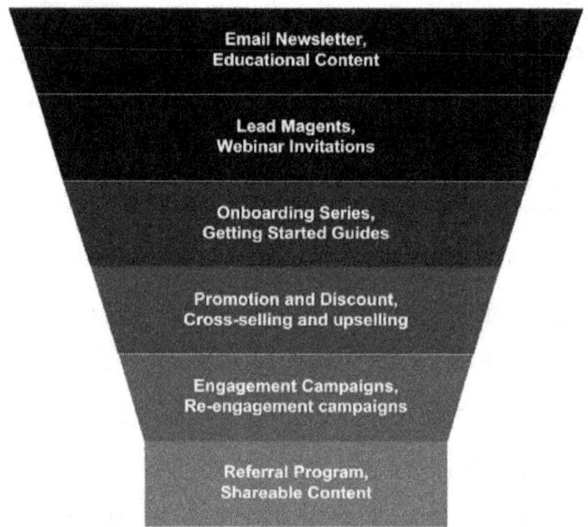

Remember, regardless of the industry, your email strategy should be tailored to your audience's preferences and needs. Personalization, segmentation, and continuous testing are key to a successful email marketing campaign.

One of the key metrics for startups is the lifetime value of the customer.

As a growth marketer, this is one of your key focus metrics.

This helps you make sense of the CAC and eventually build a profitable business.

Using Email Marketing to Increase Customer Lifetime Value (LTV) and Drive Profitability

Email marketing can help to boost LTV.

Here is how some big companies use email to improve their profitability and make sense of their CACs.

- **Amazon:** They send personalized product recommendations based on customers' browsing and purchase history. These recommendations often lead to additional purchases, increasing the overall transaction value and boosting profitability.

- **Starbucks:** They send personalized offers and discounts to their loyalty members, incentivizing them to make more purchases. This not only drives repeat business but also encourages customers to choose Starbucks over competitors.

- **Airbnb:** They send personalized emails showing properties that match the user's recent searches. This strategy increases the chances of converting potential bookings into actual reservations.

- **Dropbox:** They sent emails to existing users offering them additional storage space in exchange for referring new users. This tactic not only increased their user base but also rewarded loyal customers, enhancing their loyalty.

- **Sephora:** They send beauty tips, tutorials, and exclusive offers to their subscribers. This engagement keeps their audience connected and more likely to make repeat purchases, contributing to higher LTV.

Which Email Marketing Tools to Use?

The answer really depends on which industry and what purpose you will be using it for.

I personally use ConvertKit for my own email broadcasts and newsletter, ActiveCampaign for my SaaS clients, and Klaviyo for my ecommerce clients.

Here are some tools I recommend based on the industry and purpose:

Purpose	Email Marketing Tools	Industry
All-in-One Solutions	Mailchimp	Any Industry
	Constant Contact	Small Businesses
E-Commerce & Retail	Klaviyo	E-Commerce
	Shopify Email	Online Retail
B2B Marketing	HubSpot Email Marketing	B2B
	SendinBlue	SMBs
Personalization & Automation	ActiveCampaign	Diverse
	Drip	E-Commerce
Advanced Analytics	Campaign Monitor	Marketing Agencies
	GetResponse	Digital Marketing
Enterprise Solutions	Marketo	Enterprise
	Pardot	B2B

Chapter 23

Social Media & Influencers

Social Media is often seen as an awareness and branding channel.

First, let us break down how social media can be used across the full funnel.

This will help you see social media in a different light.

Using social media for Full Funnel Growth

Here is how it can be used effectively at each stage:

Awareness

- **Social Media Listening:** Monitor social media platforms to understand what potential customers are saying about your brand and industry. Identify trends, pain points, and interests to inform your content strategy.

- **Content Sharing:** Share engaging and informative content, including blog posts, infographics, and videos, to increase brand visibility and attract a broader audience.

- **Thematic Campaigns:** Create and promote engaging and creative themes to encourage user-generated content and increase brand awareness through social sharing.

Acquisition

- **Paid Social Media Advertising:** Utilize targeted ads on social media platforms to reach specific demographics and drive traffic to your website or landing pages.

- **Lead Generation Campaigns:** Run social media campaigns that offer valuable content or incentives in exchange for contact information, helping build a qualified lead database.

- **Influencer Marketing:** Collaborate with relevant influencers to promote your product or service, reaching their audience and driving traffic to your website.

Activation

- **Interactive Content:** Use quizzes, polls, and interactive posts to engage and convert prospects into active users or customers.

- **Social Proof:** Highlight customer testimonials and success stories to build trust and credibility, encouraging prospects to take action.

- **Social Media Customer Support:** Provide real-time support on social media to address customer queries and concerns promptly, enhancing the user experience.

Revenue

- **Product Promotions:** Run limited-time offers, discounts, or flash sales on social media to incentivize purchases and drive revenue.

- **Social Commerce:** Utilize social media platforms with integrated shopping features to facilitate direct product purchases within the platform.

- **Customer Retargeting:** Retarget previous website visitors with personalized ads on social media to encourage them to complete a purchase.

Retention

- **Community Building:** Create private groups or communities on social media where customers can engage with each other and the brand, fostering loyalty.

- **Customer Engagement:** Regularly interact with customers on social media, responding to comments and messages, and showing appreciation for their support.

- **Loyalty Programs:** Reward loyal customers with exclusive offers or early access to products through social media channels.

Referral

- **User-Generated Content (UGC) Sharing:** Encourage customers to share their experiences with your product or service through UGC, and showcase it on social media to inspire referrals.

- **Referral Contests:** Run social media contests that reward customers for referring friends, driving word-of-mouth marketing.

- **Referral Codes and Links:** Provide customers with personalized referral codes or links to share with their network, making the referral process seamless and trackable.

This shows that social media has a lot more potential for growth, than how we usually perceive it.

Yes, social media is a database.

A database you can tap into to spread the word and acquire users.

But as seen with the above methods, you can use it across the user journey.

How to select Social Media Channels?

There is a slightly different approach in which you pick your channels.

And this is true for social media as well.

Digital Marketers typically choose social media channels based on where their target audience spends the most time online.

And this makes sense.

They would focus on engaging users with organic and paid social media strategies that are brand-specific and oriented towards lead generation, conversion and building relationships with customers.

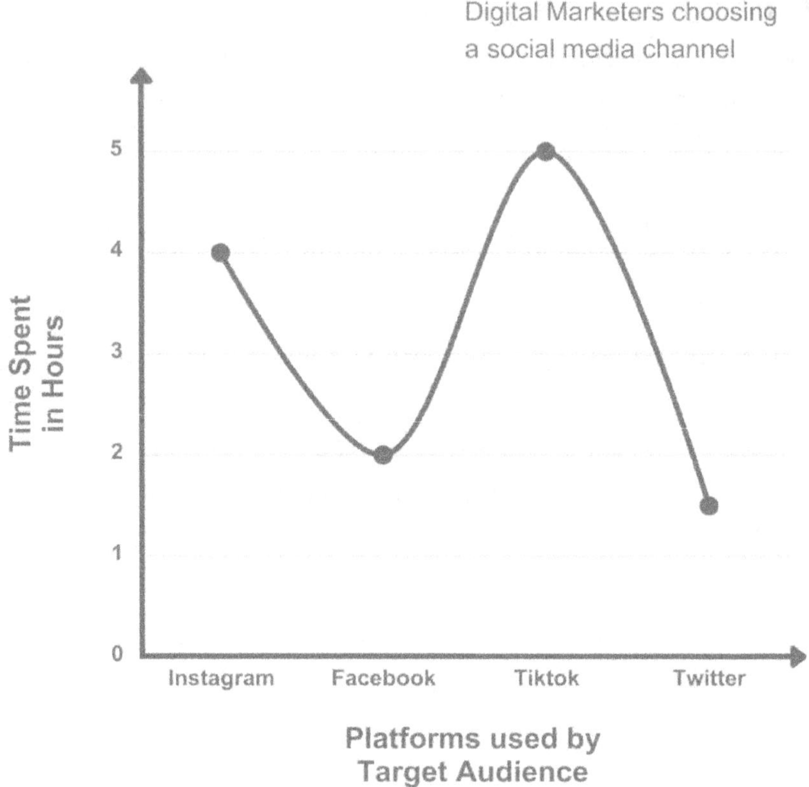

However, the approach with growth marketing is slightly different.

Of course, you want to pick channels that your audience spends time on.

But you also want to pick channels that will help you run experiment-driven testing and optimization in order to find the most efficient and scalable methods for customer acquisition and rapid growth.

As a growth marketer, you prioritize channels that show the highest potential for increased user growth and ROI, while also diversifying to protect against dependency on one or a few channels.

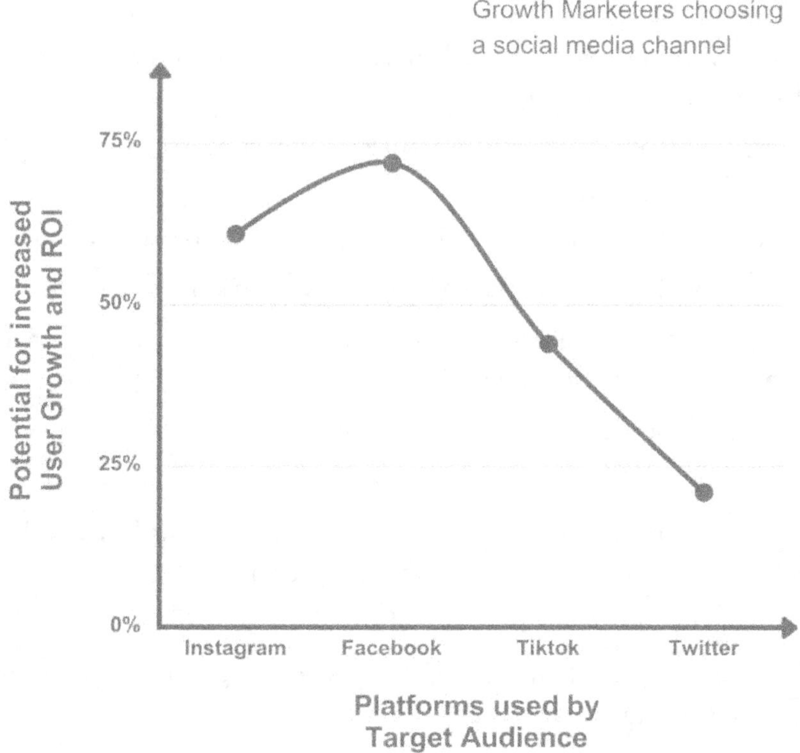

Social Media Hacks that Work on All Channels

Next, no matter which channels you pick, I am going to share hacks that will work across all channels.

The reason for this is these hacks are rooted in user psychology.

1. Creating FOMO with Urgency and Scarcity:

Create limited-time offers and exclusive deals to trigger the fear of missing out (FOMO) in your audience, encouraging them to take immediate action.

FOMO works across all channels.

2. Using Social Proof:

Display testimonials, user-generated content, and reviews to build trust and credibility among your audience, showing that others have had positive experiences with your brand.

I often provide incentives to my audience in exchange for testimonials on social media.

This is a great way to start if you do not already have social proof.

3. Influencer Marketing: (Other People's Networks)

Collaborate with influencers relevant to your niche to expand your reach and tap into their loyal followers.

We will expand on this one after this section.

4. User Polls and Surveys:

Engage your audience by seeking their opinions and feedback, making them feel valued and involved in your brand's decisions.

This also helps gather data and make decisions.

Social media is a great way for growth marketers to gather data to run experiments on other channels as well.

5. Social Contests and Giveaways:

Organize contests and giveaways to encourage user participation, boost engagement, and attract new followers.

Look for ways to have people tag and invite other people into your circle through contests.

Again, tapping into OPNs.

6. Behind-the-Scenes Content:

Share behind-the-scenes glimpses of your business to create authenticity and foster a stronger connection with your audience.

Social media is the place to be real, when everyone is trying to filter out their lives.

7. Humour and Memes:

Inject humour and share relatable memes to humanize your brand and entertain your audience.

This has been working for the longest period of time, and will continue to work.

8. Natural-looking Ads:

Create content that seamlessly integrates with the platform's user experience to avoid sounding overly promotional.

Sometimes, you do not need the most edited and highest quality ad.

You just need something people relate to.

Follow the format That is already natural to the platform.

9. Trendjacking:

Capitalize on trending topics, hashtags, and challenges to join conversations and increase your visibility.

This will give you peaks in your campaigns.

You can then repeat the process with new trends.

10. Personalization:

Tailor content and offers based on user preferences and behaviours to enhance the customer experience.

Just like personalization on your website and email campaigns, add elements of personalization into your social media channels as well.

These hacks leverage psychological principles such as social proof, scarcity, reciprocity, and emotional triggers to create engaging content and build stronger connections with your audience.

Startup Examples

Let us look at some examples of how startups leverage social media hacks we discussed above.

I have changed the names as these are from my clients, but you will now be able to spot these hacks looking at any brand account on social media That is using them.

1. Startup: Fitness App "FitX"

Hacks Used:

- **Urgency and Scarcity:** FitX ran a limited-time promotion offering a 50% discount on premium subscriptions for the first 100 sign-ups, creating a sense of urgency among potential users.

- **Influencer Marketing:** FitX collaborated with popular fitness influencers to create engaging workout challenges, attracting thousands of participants, and increasing app downloads.

- **Social Contests and Giveaways:** FitX organized a "Summer Fitness Challenge" where users could win exciting prizes by sharing their fitness progress on social media, leading to increased user-generated content and brand awareness.

2. Startup: Fashion E-commerce "Trendify"

Hacks Used:

- **Emotion-evoking Content:** Trendify shared success stories and transformation images of satisfied customers, evoking emotions and building trust among potential buyers.

- **Behind-the-Scenes Content:** Trendify offered sneak peeks of their photo shoots, design processes, and warehouse operations, giving followers a glimpse into the brand's authenticity and commitment to quality.

- **Native Advertising:** Trendify partnered with fashion influencers to seamlessly incorporate their products into stylish and trendy lifestyle posts, driving traffic to their online store.

3. Startup: Food Delivery Service "BiteDash"

Hacks Used:

- **Interactive Content:** BiteDash conducted weekly food quizzes and polls, encouraging users to vote for their favourite dishes and providing insights for menu optimization.

- **Trendjacking:** BiteDash leveraged popular food-related hashtags during national food holidays, such as #NationalPizzaDay, to promote exclusive deals and increase order volumes.

- **Customer Service:** BiteDash responded to customer queries and complaints promptly and publicly on social media, demonstrating their dedication to excellent service and customer satisfaction.

By implementing these strategies with an understanding of the psychological principles behind them, they were able to create impactful social media campaigns that contributed to their overall business growth.

Influencer Marketing

Influencers are OPNs that you can tap into.

They are one of the 4 forms of word of mouth for your business.

The other forms are advocates, affiliates, and ambassadors.

4 Forms of Word of Mouth

- **Advocates:** Satisfied customers who actively promote a brand or product to their network

- **Affiliates:** Individuals who promote a brand or product on their platforms in exchange for a commission or other incentive

- **Influencers:** Social media users with a significant following and a degree of authority in a particular industry or niche

- **Ambassadors:** Individuals who have an ongoing relationship with a brand and promote it in exchange for exclusive access to events, products, or other benefits

Typically, I suggest my clients to shortlist influencers from advocates, and to shortlist ambassadors from the influencers they worked with.

This is a natural progression.

How to Leverage Influencers

Collaborating with influencers allows startups to access new audiences, build credibility, and drive user acquisition.

Let us walk through the steps to effectively leverage influencers as OPNs for growth hacking.

- **Define Your Target Audience:** Understand your ideal customer profile and identify the niche that aligns with your product or service.

- **Research Influencers:** Use social media platforms and influencer databases to find influencers who have a significant following in your target niche.

- **Analyse Engagement:** Look for influencers with high engagement rates, as it indicates an active and engaged audience.

- **Define Your Objectives:** Determine what you want to achieve with influencer collaborations, such as increasing brand awareness, driving website traffic, or boosting sales.

- **Set Key Performance Indicators (KPIs):** Establish measurable metrics to track the success of your influencer campaigns, such as the number of clicks, conversions, or new followers.

- **Personalize Your Outreach:** Tailor your messages to each influencer, demonstrating that you have researched their content and genuinely value their collaboration.

- **Offer Value:** Provide influencers with incentives such as free product samples, exclusive access, or affiliate partnerships to create a win-win scenario.

- **Collaborate on Content Strategy:** Work with influencers to develop content that aligns with their style and resonates with their audience while conveying your brand message.

- **Highlight Benefits:** Showcase the unique value of your product or service and how it addresses the pain points of the influencer's audience.

- **Use UTM Tracking Links or Custom Discount Codes:** Provide influencers with custom tracking links or discount codes to monitor the traffic and conversions generated through their promotions.

- **Monitor KPIs:** Regularly review the performance of your influencer campaigns to gauge their impact on your growth metrics.

- **Respond to Comments:** Encourage the influencer's audience to engage with your brand by responding to comments and queries promptly.

- **Host Giveaways or Contests:** Collaborate with influencers to run giveaways or contests, increasing brand exposure and attracting new followers.

- **Repurpose UGC:** Utilize content generated by influencers and their followers in your own marketing efforts, such as featuring it on your website or social media profiles.

- **Encourage Sharing:** Motivate customers to share their experiences with your product or service, expanding your brand reach organically.

- **Nurture Relationships:** Continue building relationships with influencers beyond a single campaign, fostering loyalty and long-term collaborations.

- **Implement Ambassador Programs:** Invite influencers who consistently drive results to become brand ambassadors, offering ongoing benefits for their support.

You can also apply some of these steps while working with affiliates and ambassadors.

Chapter 24

Building Lead Generation Funnels

Contributing Author: Raj Vasani

Bio: Raj Vasani is a lead generation specialist and performance marketer based in Bangalore.

He discovered his passion for digital marketing after struggling to complete his B. Tech in IT.

Raj's journey took a defining turn when he spent his first advertising dollar on a pet store campaign, sparking his interest in performance marketing.

With a background in freelance performance marketing and managerial roles, Raj founded his agency, Campaign Coast Agency.

He is generated over $15 million in attributed revenue across diverse sectors, partnering with notable companies like Onx Homes, Bonito Designs, The Executive Center, and Yellow.ai. Additionally, he consults for agencies such as Webenza and BusinessMunim, sharing his Performance Marketing Approach.

Beyond marketing, Raj is an avid learner, delving into cooking, history, science, yoga, music, and spirituality.

He is also an active volunteer for Isha Foundation, contributing his expertise to fundraising and conservation projects, supporting rural India and environmental causes.

As you have read in this book, growth marketing is the superset of everything from the marketing landscape to the product growth ecosystem.

This chapter focuses on lead generation and performance marketing, as this is the start of everything.

As we have seen in the past chapters, and in the A3R3 funnel, it all starts with awareness.

You will constantly need new people to be aware of your product and service, and one of the most reliable and scalable ways to do that is to build performance marketing funnels.

We will be covering the aspects of performance marketing and lead generation in a phased manner.

And by the end of the chapter, what you will have is a robust system of lead generation that will make sure that you have no shortage of leads in your entire funnel of growth marketing.

Phase 1: The Research (3U Framework)

If you dive into a river without any knowledge of the water flow or the depth, there is a very high chance that you will flow away, no matter if you were a high school swimming champ.

That is why the first phase of performance marketing is research.

The core idea of this phase is the get a crystal-clear idea of:

- Understanding the Product/Service
- Understanding the Target Audience
- Understanding the Competition

Without a clear idea of the above 3 core research questions, your plan for performance marketing will be a big guessing game.

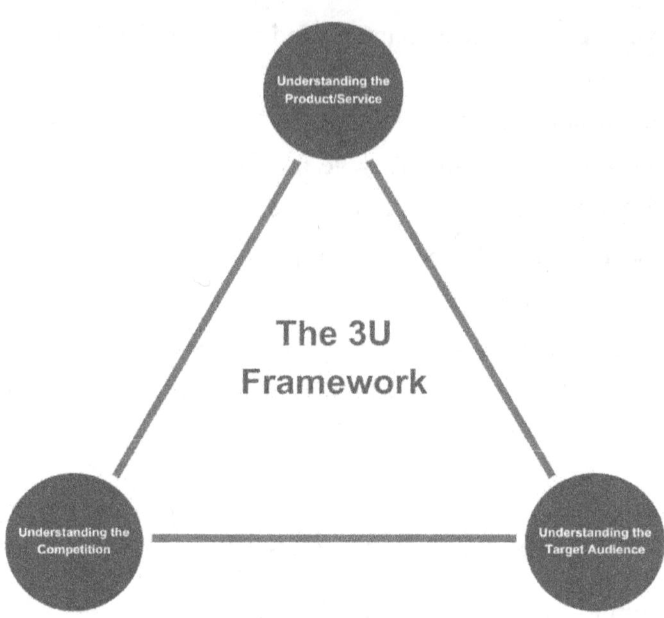

So let us look at each question and see what are the core things we need to understand for building a great lead generation campaign.

Understanding the Product

The product team will develop the product, but it is up to the marketing team to find the right message to take the product into the market.

This right message is what we call a **unique value proposition**.

Back in the 2000s in India, the deodorant market was filled with companies targeting men with the same message: *If you apply our deodorant, girls will come flying towards you.*

But in 2011, a company called FOGG came and disrupted the market.

While everyone was busy having an **Aspirational** value proposition of getting attention, FOGG came and took the route of a **Functional** value proposition by saying *"Our Spray based Deos last 24 hours"* along with a claim of 800 sprays per bottle.

Long story short, FOGG is now the market leader with a 12% market share of the Rs 3,600 crore Deodorant market in India.

That is what the right value proposition can do for your business.

Here are some categories of Value Propositions that you can take a look at while deciding the angle of messaging you would like to take:

- **Functional Value Propositions:**

  Examples:

  - o Price-based Value Proposition
  - o Quality-based Value Proposition
  - o Innovation-based Value Proposition

- **Aspirational Value Propositions:**

  Examples:

  - o Sustainability-based Value Proposition
  - o Status-based Value Proposition
  - o Social Impact Value Proposition

- **Economic Value Propositions**:

  Examples:

  - o Savings-based Value Proposition
  - o Entertainment Value Proposition

Understanding the Target Audience

Now that you know what to say, then the next step is to answer the question of "who to say to?"

The first step is to define an ICP (Ideal Customer Persona).

Traditionally, ICP was defined by key demographic features like age, location, and basic interests.

But it is not enough, and in fact, it can become counter-productive.

To give you an example, Ozzy Osbourne and Prince Charles are males, born in 1948, raised in the UK, were married twice, and are wealthy, but one is a prince of the UK while the other is the prince of darkness.

Therefore, once you have a basic idea about the target audience cleared, it is much more important to define a character.

The next step is to divide the audience into categories of how aware they are about the market.

There are 5 levels to this:

- **Level 1: Unaware**

  They are not aware of the problem nor the solution

- **Level 2: Problem Aware**

  They are aware of the problem, but they do not have the solution yet

- **Level 3: Solution Aware**

  They are aware of the problem and the solution

- **Level 4: Product Aware**

  They are aware of the exact product for their solution

- **Level 5: Most Aware**

  They are aware of the brands that have the products

Now practically speaking, your direct customer will come from Level 4 & 5, but that level of awareness is only a small segment of the entire targetable universe.

Secondly, as most businesses want direct customers, there is a huge competition you will have to face resulting in high costs of running the ads.

Level 1 audience in a way you can leave untouched as it is not worth spending time and money on them from a perspective of performance marketing, it is more suitable for branding.

But if you take a look at the Levels 2 & 3, it is a market that is left by a lot of companies as it requires initial time and money to educate them and at the same time, the market size is bigger too.

With the right communication, you can educate this audience and once they are ready to purchase, your brand is the one that they will come to given you have already helped them with nothing in return. The trust is built.

Once you combine the ICP and the Audience Awareness Levels, you have exactly the image of your ideal target audience.

Next is to understand the competitive landscape.

Understanding the Competition

When we talk about competition, we normally think of companies like us that are running the ads.

That is important, but it is needed at a later stage.

At this stage, we should identify the competition in terms of other solutions available in the market to solve the problem that you are solving and how your solution is the best one.

To do this, here is a simple exercise you should do:

- **Step 1:** List down all the alternatives that are available to your product.
    - o Mention what is bad about this particular solution.
- **Step 2:** What is the Exact Problem you are solving?
    - o Mention this the bad thing about the alternatives.
- **Step 3:** What are the implications if the problem is not solved?
    - o Mention this about the problem
- **Step 4:** What is your exact solution to the problem?
    - o Again, mention this about the problem mentioned
- **Step 5:** What are the benefits of your solution?
    - o Mention this objectively to make sure you have key points.

Here is a reference table for you:

Case: Why should an Interior design company opt for performance marketing?

Bad Alternatives	Problem Solved	Implications	Solutions	Benefits
Offline Channels and Referrals Although these can give higher quality leads it is costly with a huge issue to track the ROI. Also, the reach is limited	Reach a wide audience looking to get your services and be able to track a clear ROI of the investment	Companies would invest huge amounts and might not be able to get precise with the ROI and it will lead to them not being able to scale predictably. This will waste time and money	Lead Generation Using Performance Marketing	- Tracking and ROI - Reach a wide audience - Take data-driven steps

The more you list, the better.

Now here is a little secret trick, you can use this table to find what all things are already available in the market and use it to create your own **Unique Value Proposition.**

Congratulations on completing Phase 1.

Now Let us dive deeper into making a plan for performance marketing.

Phase 2: The Funnel

In the last phase, we spoke of the Levels of Audience Awareness and we saw the biggest opportunity lies in targeting the Level 2 & 3 Audiences.

This is why creating a funnel is important.

Some of the most common funnels are:

Webinar Funnels

- You bring people for a free webinar, using traffic channels, nurture them with email and other channels like Whatsapp (based on your market), and pitch your product/service on the webinar.
- Suitable for 1 to many selling.

Lead Generation Funnels

- You bring people by using a lead magnet that is closely related to the product/service you have.

- Using Nurture channels, you deliver them more value along with the lead magnet.

- Then you pitch them the product directly (if low cost) or get on a call with them to sell the product (if high cost).

Tripwire Funnels

- It is similar to the lead generation funnel, but over here, instead of giving away a lead magnet for free, you sell them a low-cost product (ideally high in value).

- This gives customers a taste of what your products are like and then you upsell them high-cost products.

Email Nurture Funnels

- You get people to subscribe to your email newsletter and then provide them value constantly without asking for anything in return.

- This funnel is not developed to sell directly but instead to build unbreakable trust with your potential customers.

- Eventually you promote your products to them as a recommendation in an organic way.

If you take a close look at each funnel, you will see 2 core parts that work together to bring in leads, nurture them and turn them into a customer:

- **Traffic:** This is where you run ads to generate leads.

- **Nurture:** This is where you talk to the leads and educate them.

As a performance marketer, your job is to take care of both the core elements, but Traffic is your main domain.

In the nurture part, you are supposed to help with the communication approach. Because you are aware of the communication that works on the ads to generate leads in the first place.

See we will do a deeper dive into traffic channels and get an overview of nurture channels.

Traffic

First and foremost, thing is to identify the channels where your target audience hangs out.

You already have completed the audience research, you based on their behaviour, you can easily identify the channels they prefer.

Ideally, for B2C lead generation, audiences are available to target on:

- Meta (Facebook & Instagram)
- Google (& YouTube)

There are other platforms too, but Meta & Google have a major share of the audiences that you are looking for.

Unless you are able to crack these 2, there is no point in discussing anything else.

Once you have decided on the channel, you need to plan for each channel individually.

Meta Ads

Meta ads are a Social Media Advertising channel.

While planning Meta ads, you need to take care of 3 things:

- Campaign Objective and Structure
- Target Audience
- Ads and Creatives

Campaign Objective and Structure

As a performance marketer, your key objective will be to generate leads or sales. Thus, you should directly go for Leads or Sales as the campaign objective.

When you are generating leads, Meta gives you many options to capture leads like an Instant Form or Website or Messenger or a direct call.

When you are having a funnel, it is best to use a website landing page.

Website conversion ads will give you a better quality of the lead and at the same time, you can automate a lot of things to start communicating with the leads as you have full control of your website.

A few years ago, Meta was relying more on the interests and targeting more, thus it was recommended to have a complex ads structure with multiple campaigns and ad sets.

But now, with the increasing reliance on AI and ML, it is best to have a simple campaign structure and focus more on Ads and Creatives which we will explore in the coming sections.

So, it is best to follow the below structure:

1 Campaign with 2-5 Audiences targeting based on themes and each ad set having 2-3 creatives.

Meta has 2 types of strategies to allocate budgets, 1 is at the campaign level and another is at the ad group level.

My preference is to keep the budgets at the campaign level which is called CBO (campaign budget optimization) as it gives more power to the AI to take the decision.

You can use ABO (ad set budget optimization) if you want to control the spending manually on every ad set.

ABO is good to do testing of the audience with, but if you are looking to make a campaign that will scale, CBO will be your best friend.

Now Let us take a look at setting up the target audiences.

Target Audience

Gone are the days of doing single interest-based targeting. Meta is becoming smart and it is time to leverage it.

Instead of going with unique interests, it is better to club interests based on themes.

These themes are developed based on the type of audience you are going after.

For example, if you have a luxury interior design product, you can target based on below themes:

- **Direct Interior Based Interests**

  Sample Interests:

  - Interior Design
  - Kitchens
  - Architecture

- **Luxury Products Based Interests**

  Sample Interests:

  - Luxury Fashion Products
  - Luxury Vehicles
  - Luxury Activities

- **HNI Behaviour Based Interests**

  Sample Interests:

  - Frequent International Travel
  - First Class Tickets
  - Plays Golf

One thing to keep in mind is to make sure that the audience overlap is less than 30%, else it is better to combine the audiences into a single ad set.

Along with this, you should use the details of your ICP to have the age, location, and gender added too.

Ads and Creatives

The key thing to keep in mind while planning is that a user of Facebook or Instagram is not actively searching for a product or service.

They are spending their time engaging with the world; thus, your ads have to interrupt their pattern and capture attention.

You also need to see what kind of ads are already working for your close competitors.

So first, you should do a quick competitor research using **Meta Ads Library.**

Search your competitors and see some of their oldest ads (because if they are running an ad for 1-2 months, that means the audience is engaging with the ads)

Over here, take note of these things:

- What is the type of creative they are using? (Single Image, Carousel, Video)

- What is the messaging they have on the ads?

- What is the value proposition they are highlighting?

Once you have this information, you will know what type of creative to make and what messaging to have. Combine it with your unique value proposition and voila, your creativity is ready.

Here are some important things to keep in mind while making your ads:

- Make sure that your ads are interrupting the Pattern of organic feed.

    - This is achieved using eye-catching image elements or video transitions.

- Call out the problem you are solving or the target audience within the first 5 seconds of the ads.

- Use the Problem - Solution - Value Proposition Framework to make your ads

- Add multiple Primary text and headlines for your creatives.

    - Meta allows up to 5, so have at least three variations.

- Have creatives for all placements

    - 1:1 for Feed placement on Facebook

    - 4:5 for Feed placement on Instagram

    - 9:16 for Story and Reels placement on both the platforms

    - 1.19:1 for other placements like Facebook right column and in-article ads

With all this information at your disposal, it is best to create 2-3 ads with a unique angle but the same value proposition.

For this, you can go back to the 3rd U of your research.

In the Competitor Analysis Sheet, we have mentioned what are the problems we are solving along with our solutions and benefits.

You can combine these elements and create multiple communication approaches for a single product or service.

Next, let us take a look at Google as a lead generation channel.

Google Ads

Contrary to Meta Ads, Google is an intent-driven channel, which means people are actively searching for their problems, solutions, and products.

The intent of leads from Google is comparatively higher compared to social ad channels like Meta.

Thus, it is one of the most loved channels by your competition too.

So, the first step is to see what is the competitive landscape on Google.

For this, you can use tools like SEMrush and Spyfu.

You will be able to find which competitors are running ads on Google and the keywords they are currently bidding on.

This will give you an idea of seed keywords that are working in the market already and later you can use these to do further keyword research and find more keywords.

Now coming to Google Search Ads, there are many levers you can use to get the best results.

But to set up a complete Google search ad campaign, you need the below-mentioned things:

- Keyword Research
- Campaign Structure
- Negative Keywords List
- Ad Copies and Ad Assets

Let us take a look at each of these.

Keyword Research

As the name suggests, it is research, so make sure you put in enough time to gather as many targetable keywords as possible.

Side-Note*: I recommend you perform this activity every 3 months to see what all new keywords are available to target.*

My go-to tools for keyword research are "Keywords Planner" and "SEMrush."

In the beginning, when I was just getting started, I only used Keywords Planner by Google. It is good enough, but with SEMrush, you can identify the intent of the keywords as well.

If you do not have SEMrush, do not worry, you will be able to figure out the intent mostly through common sense, and if you are confused about any keyword, just do a quick Google search for it, and check the SERP results.

Based on the results, you will be able to identify how Google is treating the keyword.

Below is how SEMrush defines the intent:

Navigational Keywords: The user searches for a specific website. Ex: Canva Website	**Information Keywords:** The user searches for information on a topic Ex: What is a good design tool?
Commercial Keywords: The user researches options for a product or a service Ex: Canva VS Adobe	**Transactional Keywords:** The user searches for a specific product or brand. Ex: Buy Canva premium

We can relate the Keyword intent with the Audience's Awareness Levels:

Level 2 & 3 Audience: Informational Keywords

Level 4 & 5 Audience: Commercial and Transactional Keywords

One thing to keep in mind is that people who are searching for information on google are not in the mode of purchase or enquire, so make sure you are promoting your informational lead magnets to them on search ads.

To the Level 4 & 5 audience, you can promote your product/services or your lead magnets too.

So, the next set is to take the seed keywords and put them on the Google keywords planner.

Once you do that, you will find hundreds if not thousands of keywords that you can target.

To filter the keywords, follow these steps:

- They should be relevant
- They should have a good search volume (At least 50-100)
  - If you are in a category with low search volume then add more keywords <50 volume too
- High-intent keywords usually have competitor running ads on them, so select those too.
- You should have a budget to suffice the keyword's volumes and bids
  - Do an average of the top bid (low range) and (high range) for each keyword.
  - Multiply the above by the search volume.
  - This will give you possible monthly spending on that keyword.
  - Now add all the keywords possible monthly spend and that will give you an idea of the monthly budget required.

    Note: This is my method to get an estimation, but based on the actual performance of the campaign, I change the allocation in real time

Once you have a refined keyword list, now we must develop themes of these keyword sets.

Each theme becomes a unique ad group for us.

For example: Let us say you are selling trading and stock market books, based on the above method, you can filter the keywords.

You can bifurcate the keywords based on the below themes.

Note: Try to have a max 8 keywords per theme for ease of management.

Theme	Keyword
Trading Books	trading books
	option trading books
	best trading books
	best book for options trading
	simple trading book
	intraday trading books
	for beginners
Stock investing Books	stock market books
	share market books
	stock market books for beginners
	best stock market books for beginners
	books on Indian stock market

Great! Now you know how to do keyword research and what are the factors that help in theming as well as budgeting.

The next step is campaign structure!

Campaign Structure

After keyword research, this is the most important part of setting up a campaign.

Ideally, for any type of business, we need to have a campaign structure that is divided into 3 segments:

- **Brand Campaign:** This campaign has brand keywords in targeting, to make sure competitors are not able to come on top for our brand.

- **Product/service Campaign:** These are the keywords that people will search to get your products/services. We just did keyword research for the same.

- **Competitor Campaign:** These are the brand keywords of your competitors. You want this as a separate campaign to have the best control of the spending and targeting.

Now you can have multiple Product/Service Based Campaigns as well.

What keyword match types should I keep for the keywords?

Well, if it is a new account, my personal recommendation would be to go with phrase match for all your product/service-based keywords.

The reason for this is that with phrase match, you reach sufficient variations of your target keywords while also making sure that you do not show up for totally bad keywords which will come from broad match.

For your competitor keywords, go with exact match keywords only, because in my experience, when using phrase or broad, you can get many costly clicks and still not get good conversions.

For brand keywords, go with 1 ad group of exact match keywords and 1 ad group with a broad match.

Negative keywords

In the Google ads account, we have 3 levels of negative keywords possible:

- **Account Level:** These negatives basically do not make sense for your business at all!

- **Campaign Level:** These are to make sure that your targeting does not collide with any of your other campaigns and also the targeting is focused on your actual objective of the campaign.

- **Ad Group Level:** These negatives should be used to make sure that campaign hygiene is maintained based on your campaign structure.

Side note: *Even though Google says that keywords do not fight against other keywords in the same account, cross-negative keywords help you maintain the overall hygiene of the campaigns.*

Ad Copies and Assets

By now, you have your campaign structure and keywords ready

Let us combine all of this and make killer ad copies and assets.

Thumb-rule: Use all the allocated spaces available on your ads account.

For RSA, we have 15 headlines, 4 descriptions, and 2 display paths.

Here is a simple framework you can follow:

- **5 Headlines:** Insert the target keywords

- **5 Headlines:** Product/service features, USP, value proposition, Brand, etc.

- **5 Headlines:** CTAs or some indication of what to expect on the landing page

- **2 Descriptions:** Crisp copy about the brand, products, and services with keywords inserted

- **2 Descriptions:** Your offer, USPs and CTAs

- **Display Path 1:** Offer

- **Display Path 2:** CTA

There are in total 12 assets available. You need to make sure you are using all possible assets.

Below are key assets you will need to take care of

- **Sitelinks:** Make them extremely relevant and support anything that you say on the main ad copy

- **Callout:** As the name suggests, call out your USPs and Features here

- **Structured Snippet:** Highlight the key aspects of your products/services here

- **Call:** If you can take calls, then do add this!

- **Lead Form:** This makes it easier for you to collect the leads

- **Images:** Add them for higher relevance and CTRs

- **Location:** If you are a local business then make sure you have the office or business location mentioned here.

Now that the 2 core Traffic channels are ready Let us take a look at the Nurture Channels to start communicating with the leads.

Nurture

Just like the traffic channels, there are multiple nurture channels too but mainly, email, SMS, WhatsApp, and calls are used.

SMS and Calls are more suitable for inquiries and notifications but you can use emails and WhatsApp as notifications as well as nurturing channels.

As previously mentioned, as a performance marketer, your major role is to work on the traffic channels and generate qualified leads.

But at the same time, you should play a role in deciding the communication that happens when a lead is generated, as you are the one that has spoken with the user using your ads, showcase the product as a solution for their problems using the landing page and convert them into a lead.

Let us take a look at the communication approach.

Communication Approach

One of the major reasons funnels fails is that the communication is inconsistent throughout the customer journey.

Imagine this, you want to get fit, and while scrolling through Instagram, you see an ad by a fitness company that says, "Gym routine guide to lose 10 kgs in a month - Download for Free".

It matches perfectly with your intent of getting fit, and you sign-up for it.

The moment you sign up, you showed your interest in getting information about Routines, but you have not enquired to sign up for the Gym.

You receive an email with the guide, and the moment you open the guide, you see it is the basic routine structured well, but throughout the guide, they are promoting their health supplements only.

There is no value you received. Imagine the dis-taste you would feel for the company.

To make matters worse, in 2 days, you receive a phone call from the same company to sell you the supplements.

I do not think that you would ever like to get a message from the company in the future.

Contrary to this, let us assume that the guide was on point, and it really had amazing routines that can help people lose weight.

You started following it, and within 1 month, you lost around 6 Kg. Along with the guide, they were constantly sending you motivational messages as well as FAQs via email for 1 month.

You would be ecstatic and the trust that is built with the company is unbreakable.

Then after 1 month, let us say they give you a survey form on your experience of the last 30 days, and once you fill it, they ask for consent to send you more routines and products to help you improve your fitness.

After your consent, they call you up, upsell their products and fitness programs, and you will be showering them with money because of the trust.

In both cases, the audience was the same, and the lead magnet was the same but the communication post generating a lead, changed the game.

That is the power of right communication.

Below is 1 matrix that will be your guiding light to decide the communication approach based on your audience's level of intent and awareness.

LOW	INTENT					HIGH
A W A R E N E S S	Audience	Communication	Audience	Communication	Audience	Communication
	Prospect not aware of your	Brand Awareness	Prospect is NOT aware of	Brand Awareness Problem	Prospect NOT aware	Brand Awareness Problem

business and is NOT in-market for your solution	Problem Awareness	your business but is potentially in-market	Awareness	of your business but IS in-market	Awareness Solution Awareness
Prospect is aware of your business but NOT in-market	Problem Awareness	Prospect is aware of your business and potentially in-market	Problem Awareness Solution Awareness	Prospect is aware of your business and IS in-market	Solution Awareness
HIGH Prospect knows your business very well but is NOT in-market	Problem Awareness Solution Awareness	Prospect knows your business very well and is potentially in-market	Problem Awareness Solution Awareness	Prospect knows your business very well and IS in-market	Solution Awareness

Using the above matrix, you can decide the level of audience you would like to reach out to and what type of communication you should have with them.

Chapter 25

Executing Performance Marketing Campaigns

Contributing Author: Raj Vasani

Phase 3: The Execution

Phew…We have come a long way! The research is ready, and the plan and funnel are ready. Now we need to take a look at the execution-level stuff.

Landing Pages

This is one element of the funnel that has the potential to make or break the entire machine.

Consider landing pages as your shop where customers are coming constantly to check out your product. Imagine if your store is dirty, or some of the demo products do not work at all, or in the worst-case scenario, your sales rep is not attentive.

It will not only make the customer leave, but also, it will create a negative brand image.

Having said that, you do not need a landing page developed by designers and coders of Google or Microsoft.

A basic landing page with no broken elements will do the job because the heavy lifting of generating a lead is done by your landing page copy.

No surprise that expert copywriters can charge up to $1000 per 500 words for a landing page copy.

Let us take a look at what makes a landing page great!

For this, we will divide the landing page into 3 sections:

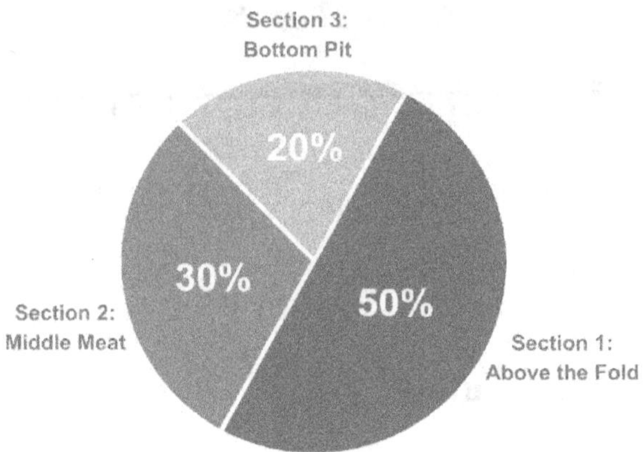

Section 1: Above the Fold - The Emotional Trigger

This section is visible the moment you open the landing page. Statistically, ~80% of the users bounce from the landing page if they do not connect with this section.

So, the majority of the efforts need to be towards this section only.

This section must have the below-mentioned elements (at least):

- **Headline**: The headline aims to explain your unique value proposition and the outcome for the audience.

- **Sub-Headline:** A single-liner explanation as to how you plan to do it. Justify the headline's promise.

- **Give visual aid:** Add a video that explains everything about your offering, and if you do not have a video, then add an image to assist the headline and sub-headline in putting your point through.

- **Add Social Proof:** You do not have to clutter the section with testimonials, but add any social proof you can here. For example, 4.5/5 stars on Google/ Trustpilot.

- **Provide a Strong CTA:** Add a button or a form for them to fill in the information. Use a clever copy on the button that aligns with every other element. Do not be lazy to write "Sign Up."

Now what kind of messaging will you have in this Section?

Your messaging should bring out the emotions of the user and also make sure that it matches the ad that you have created.

Humans make purchasing decisions emotionally and then justify them logically.

If you want to purchase a car, you will find the car which you like the most and connect with. Then you find out about the engine power, fuel efficiency, etc. to justify your purchase.

That justification comes in the next section.

Section 2: Middle Meat - The Logical Justification

As the name suggests, it is the middle meat!

It needs to have all the juicy information about your product/services and it should answer some basic questions:

- What exactly will a user get?
- Why is this solution the best for the problem you are trying to solve?
- How does this product/service work?
- Who has it worked for in the past?

You must be creative here by using visual elements to keep the page engaging. Else this part is skipped by most of the people.

Section 3: Bottom Pit - The Last Attempt

Majority of the people who end up in this section are quick scrollers, they do not read a lot and scroll down to find "what else?" mainly.

So, this section ideally should be like a quick summary section where you are explaining whatever you have mentioned so far in a brief way.

This is your last attempt to get the lead. Keep the communication crisp and to the point along with a strong CTA.

Apart from these sections, landing pages must have some Conversion Rate Optimization elements to capture the leads and attention of the users like:

- **Chatbot**: It is a great element to have on your landing page. It is like an always active sales rep who is trained by you to answer any doubt a user may have before becoming a lead.

- **Exit Intent Pop-Up:** Tools available would bring a pop-up on the screen if it senses that a user is about to leave the page. You can use this as the final attempt to capture the lead.

- **Notification Pop-Up:** Tools like Nidgify are great for giving social proof on the landing pages and increase FOMO. It shares live notifications of the purchases or leads filled by other users on the landing page.

- **Calculator and Quizzes:** People like to engage with interactive elements on a landing page. By building a calculator or a quiz related to your product, you can engage users and subtly mention how your product can help them based on the inputs they gave. You can ask for the lead details to access the results of the quiz or the calculator.

To measure the impact of your landing page and CRO efforts, use tools like Hotjar or Microsoft Clarity. These tools provide you heatmaps and sessions recordings to see the sections where a user spends more time or bounces from.

All the above information will help you to create very high-converting landing pages. But as a performance marketer, your role is not to bring a huge volume of leads but these leads should be relevant to the business too.

This is where your landing page forms come in.

When you go live with the campaigns, you need to sit with the sales team or business owner and understand the factors on the basis of which they will mark the lead as a qualified lead.

Using these factors, you can develop a form that does not ask just the contact details but also asks certain qualifying questions too.

On top of that, many times, people tend to give wrong contact information, so you can set up OTP verification using email or phone number as well to make sure you are getting interested prospects with correct information only.

Now that the landing page is ready Let us look at lead tracking infrastructure.

Conversion Tracking, Attribution, and Automation

Before even thinking about launching a campaign, there has to be a clear setup of tracking, attribution, and automation, which is tested thoroughly at every stage for any possible error.

Because if you do not know where your customers are coming from out of all the leads that are generated, it will be a harakiri, and you will not understand which channel/campaign/targeting/ad is working to bring you business.

Leading you to keep spending money on everything.

So let us tackle every point individually, starting with Conversion Tracking.

Conversion Tracking

This is unique to the platform you are running the ads on and the funnel stages you might have.

But the core principle is to track every important action from a user to a lead to a customer.

This will be best explained using an example.

Let us say you are going with a webinar funnel to generate leads.

So, this is how the journey goes:

Ads ▶ Landing Page ▶ Thank You Page ▶ Webinar Show-up ▶ Purchase Confirmation

If we take a look at it, the important events that trigger here are:

- **A user viewed the ad and clicked on it**: This is already tracked inside the ads platforms automatically.

- **The user viewed the landing page:** This is an event that is outside of the platform and needs to be tracked. But this is not a conversion for us. Therefore, it should not be marked as a conversion.

- **The user filled out the lead form and got re-directed to the thank you page:** This is a conversion for you, so you need to install a conversion code that will trigger on page load.

- **Lead shows up on Webinar and purchases the product:** On the payment page that you provide them, you can set up a redirect to a page. This page only opens when a purchase is made. You need to track this as a purchase conversion action, but it should not be your optimizing event.

The last event is just to pass the actual purchase data to the platforms in order to create lookalike audiences or see which campaign is contributing to sales directly from the campaigns.

Now that you understand the type of events that are to be tracked Let us take a look at the best practices at Channel Level.

Meta Ads Best Conversion Practises:

1. **Define Clear Conversion Goals:** Like the example above, you should be clear as to which event is a lead for you, and which event is a purchase. So clearly define these goals before setting up conversion tracking.

2. **Utilize the Facebook Pixel:** Implement the Facebook Pixel on your website. This tracking code helps you track user interactions and behaviours, allowing you to measure and optimize for conversions.

3. **Use Conversion API**: The world is moving towards cookie-less marketing. With so many cookie blockers and consent as well as IOS devices having the option to block cookies at a large scale, it is difficult to track everything perfectly using pixel tracking. Thus, using Conversion API, you are using server-side tracking

instead of browser-based tracking, ensuring 99% percent of the events are tracked properly.

4. **Assign Values to Conversions:** This may not be relevant to every business but if you are in a business which is having clear monetary value defined for every action, then you should track that as well along with the conversions.

Google Ads Best Conversion Practises:

1. **Define Clear Conversion Goals:** Similar to Meta, clearly understand the events that matter for your business.

2. **Use Campaign Level Goals:** Google by default, will mark every conversion that you set up as an account-level conversion. It is best to mark every conversion as a campaign-level conversion and assign it to the campaign's manual for optimization.

3. **Use Enhanced Conversion:** Google too is tracking to pass as much data to the algorithms for better optimization. So along with the basic conversion setup, the enhanced conversion feature supplements your existing conversion data by sending hashed first-party customer data in a privacy-safe way.

4. **Mark unimportant events as secondary conversion:** Google allows you to bring more data into the platform for your observation. Mark any conversion as a secondary conversion that you would like to track but do not give it to the algorithm as optimization data. For example: view products.

5. **Assign Values to Conversions:** This is the same concept as Meta.

Once you have everything set, please check every conversion action thoroughly.

You can use Google tag assistance to check for Google and Meta has it is built feature to test events in the events overview section.

Let us move to attribution.

Attribution

There are many tools and systems that you can use for having clear attribution. But for the scope of this book, we will be taking a look at using UTM parameters to track the leads and attribution of sales.

Now what is a UTM parameter?

A UTM parameter is a short piece of text you add to a website link to help you keep track of where your website visitors are coming from.

It is like a special code that gives you information about your marketing efforts.

UTM parameters are super useful because they help you determine which ads or campaigns are bringing in the most people and which marketing channels are working the best.

Generally, A UTM parameter has a few parts:

- **Source (utm_source):** This tells you where the traffic is coming from, like if it is from a Google or Meta.

- **Medium (utm_medium):** This says what kind of marketing it is, like if it is from a paid ad, an organic search, or a social media post.

- **Campaign (utm_campaign):** This helps you tell apart different campaigns or promotions. So, if you are running a brand and competitor campaigns, you can use different campaign names to see how well they are doing.

- **Term (utm_term):** This one is mainly for paid search ads. It helps you know which specific keyword triggered the ad. But you can use it for Meta ads to pass the information regarding the targeting theme you used.

- **Content (utm_content):** This helps you distinguish different ads within the same campaign. For example, if you took two different communication approaches in the same campaign, this UTM parameter will help you identify which one is working in terms of the sales post generating the leads.

When someone clicks on a link with UTM parameters, the info goes to your analytics tool like Google Analytics.

But as we are talking about utilizing it for sales attribution, you can pass this data to your CRM or sheet where you are storing the lead information.

Once you have some customers out of the leads, you can check which UTMs those customers have and attribute the sales to that platform, campaign, targeting, and ads.

Alright, then let us move on to the last part of this section, which is Automation.

Automation

Automation is now as wide as an ocean and simple too.

All you need is an automation tool like Pabbly or Zapier, and there is nothing you cannot do.

For the scope of performance marketing, we will talk about the must-have automation.

Again, this may change according to the type of funnel and flow you created to generate a lead and turn them into a paying customer.

But more or less, the below-mentioned automation will sort your customer journey.

Here is a thumb rule for every automation: *Any message you share should match your ad, offer, & landing page.*

- **Welcome Message when a Lead is Generated**

  The moment a lead is generated, they should receive a communication from you. Use this message as an opportunity to welcome them or share with them the lead magnet they signed up for.

  Channels That Can Be Used:

  o   Emails

  o   WhatsApp

- o   Auto Phone Calls

- **Nurture Sequence post welcome message:**

Once you have sent them a welcome message, do not ghost them ever. Provide them with more and more value but at the same time, do not overdo it to annoy them away. This is a place to build a connection with them.

Channels That Can Be Used:

- o   Emails | Ideal Frequency: 2-3/week

- o   Whatsapp | Ideal Frequency: 1/week

  - *Note: Whatsapp is a heavily checked platform, so if your prospects are not engaging with your messages, reduce the frequency.*

- o   Live Calls | Ideal Frequency: 1/month

  - This is not a compulsory step, but if you have constantly new leads coming into your system, you can do a live call to everyone to build a connection and help them out.

  - Restrain from doing it more frequently as it will only reduce the value of your time from their perspective. Have an element of exclusivity.

- **Notifications and Reminders:**

If you are doing a webinar, workshop, online event, etc. it is best to have a system to increase the excitement of the audience.

Email Automation:

- o   Send an email 2 days before the event as a reminder and showcase all things you will cover.

- o   Send an email 1 day before the event and showcase the testimonials of the people who attended the event previously.

Whatsapp Automation:

o   Send a message 1 day before the event as a reminder, keep the messages short and to the point.

o   Send a message on the day of the event as a reminder.

o   Send a message 2 hours before the event

o   Send a reminder 15 minutes before the event

o   Send a message once the event is on

Phone Automation

o   Give an automated call reminder just one time before the event, ideally 2 hours before.

These mentioned automations are just a few of the possible automation that you can do.

Once you have a funnel ready, always be on the lookout for any step which can be automated and make sure it is automated. This takes away human interaction which brings consistency and reduces errors.

Now that you have the conversion tracking, attribution, and automation set, spend a good amount of time testing the flow.

Ensure every data point is passed to the right platforms for the next steps to trigger automatically.

We are set to go live now, let us take a quick look to ensure we have everything before hitting the publish button.

Campaign Execution Checklist

General:

- Landing Page is working
- Form Redirects to the thank you page upon completion
- Conversions trigger on the thank you page
- Automated welcome message delivered upon lead form completion.

Meta:

- Correct objective is selected for the campaigns

- ABO/CBO is selected thoughtfully and budget is added correctly
- Correct lead capture destination is selected (Landing Page / Native Form Etc.)
- Correct pixel and optimization event selected
- Audience Setup is correct
- Advantage+ Placements selected
- Right creatives are selected in sizes for all placements
- Correct ad copies are added without any spelling errors
- Right Landing Page URL is added with UTM Parameters
- Correct Facebook Page and Instagram Profile is selected to run the ads

Google:

- Correct objective is selected
- Correct Channel is selected (Search, discovery, etc)
- Correct campaign level goals are selected for optimization
- Preferred bidding strategy selected
- Right Location is selected
- Correct budget is added
- All keywords are added based on themes with preferred match types
- Unique RSA ads added for each ad group
- RSA having Good or above ad strength
- Correct landing page URLs selected along with UTM parameters
- Negative keywords added

That covers most of the steps you will need to take while setting up your campaigns.

Now that the campaigns are executed, you will start seeing a lot of data and numbers. The role of performance marketers is to take a look at these numbers and find optimization opportunities to improve campaign performance.

Right from the reach and impressions to clicks, lead, and eventually to a customer.

There are a lot of moving parts, but numbers tell the story that you should be able to read.

That brings us to this chapter's last phase (and the un-ending phase), Optimizations.

Phase 4: The Optimizations

The core part of understanding optimizations is to know your metrics right.

Each data point is related to some or the other selection that you have done in the planning and execution phase.

But below mentioned are the key metrics that you must have track of.

CPM (Cost Per Thousand Impressions)

The cost to show your ads 1000 times. This is extremely relevant for Meta ads as this is how you are charged for your ads.

This metric depends on the audience that you have as well as the relevancy of the ad to the audience.

So, if you feel that your CPMs are increasing then it is an indication that you need to work on improving your audience as well as testing creatives with the existing audience.

Frequency (Impressions / Reach)

This metric indicates the number of times a single person sees your ads. It is calculated by dividing the impressions by unique reach.

An increasing frequency is an indication of your audience seeing the same creative and messaging multiple times, thus you should work on getting new creatives.

Also here is something that I have observed, as the frequency increases the cost of ads also increases, thus if your frequency is around 3, it is time to find another winning creative to make sure that your audience is not developing blindness to your ads.

Again, this metric is more important on Meta than Google Search.

CPC (Cost Per Click)

As CPM is the metric basis on which Meta charges you, CPC is the metric basis on which Google charges you.

So essentially, you only pay for the clicks that you receive on Google, irrespective of how many impressions you receive.

Thus, it is the core metric for Google, but at the same time, it is important on Meta too.

CTR (Click Through Rate)

The percentage of people who clicked on your ad after seeing it. This metric gives you a clear indication of how relevant you are messaging and the creative is to the audience that you are targeting.

LP view rate (Landing page view rate)

The percentage of people who clicked on the ad and viewed the landing page. This gives you an indication of the % drop that happens when your landing page is loading.

This is a low-hanging fruit to fix as it can be fixed technically.

Conversion Rate

The percentage of people that converted for your desired action like filling the form out of total landing page views.

This is what we do CRO (conversion rate optimization) which we discussed in the landing page section.

You can see conversion rates as high as 70% with the right offer, messaging, and traffic.

So always keep in mind to test more and more ideas to improve your conversion rates.

CPA (Cost Per Action aka Cost Per Conversion)

This is the cost to acquire one conversion.

More often than not, this is going to be your key metric to optimize for.

I have seen cases where CTRs and CPMs are not the best, but that campaign and ad have the lowest cost per conversion.

So do not consider each metric separately, systematically view them and make sense of the total data.

Open Rates (Emails and Whatsapp)

The percentage of recipients who open your email and messages.

This metric is directly related to your subject line on the email. So, if you feel the scope of improvement, work on testing multiple subject lines.

Click-Through Rate (Emails)

If you are adding links inside your emails, then CTR is the percentage of recipients who clicked on links within your email. To improve this number, you need to ensure that the email's body is pushing the reader to click the links.

CAC (Customer Acquisition Cost)

It is a metric that measures the cost a business incurs to acquire a new customer. So as a performance marketer, at the end of the day, you need to calculate this number to see the real profitability of your campaigns.

ROAS (Return on Ad Spend)

The revenue generated for every buck spent on advertising. This gives you an idea of how your campaigns are performing with respect to the top-line revenue.

Once you have a hang on these metrics, you will be able to find gaps across the entire flow of user -> lead -> customer and you will be able to do optimizations wherever needed.

These optimizations will be different for each platform and every funnel but using the above metrics, you will be able to see what you need to do to improve the performance.

As I have mentioned, this phase of performance marketing is a never-ending process.

With every change you make, you spend some time seeing the impact of it. Positive or negative, you need to measure the changes objectively.

And as you might have read from other places too. The key to improving performance is to do only 3 things:

Test, Test, and Test.

The above two chapters were contributed by Raj Vasani.

Chapter 26

SEO Hacking

Contributing Author: Sanjay Shenoy

Bio: Sanjay Shenoy is the creator of the SEO Career Kickstarter program and a partner at Boring Marketing, a global SEO agency.

He has been in the SEO space and has worked with clients like Zerodha, Mercedes Benz India, Thrillophilia, Yourstory and more and helped get exponential results with SEO.

Driven by my life-transforming journey with SEO, he has also trained more than 1,000 people and helped them build their careers in SEO.

While he is not doing SEO, you can catch him training in Muay Thai, watching Formula 1, listening to great music, and giving belly rubs to his dog, Max.

Introduction to SEO

SEO, the art, and science of convincing search engines like Google to recommend your content as the top solution to user queries, revolves around one key objective: solving problems.

It transcends mere rankings and organic traffic, prioritizing users' needs.

To achieve this, we must comprehend how search engines function. A simple analogy can help us grasp the concept better.

Imagine a librarian who carries out three primary functions:

Step 1: Gathering as many books as possible.

Step 2: Organizing the books into various genres like fiction, romance, crime, and children's literature.

Step 3: Recommending a suitable book to readers based on their requirements and the library's collection.

Similarly, search engines perform three key functions: crawling, indexing, and ranking.

Crawling: Search engine robots explore the web for fresh and updated content.

Indexing: Google comprehends and organizes page content during indexing.

Ranking: Google evaluates around 200 signals to rank pages based on relevance, authority, and user signals. While not all ranking factors are disclosed, we can categorize them into three main groups using the RAU framework:

- **Relevancy:** How well does your content align with users' search queries?

- **Authority:** Among the relevant results, how credible and authoritative is your content?

- **User Signals:** How do users engage with and trust your content?

Though Google recommends the EEAT (Experience, Expertise, Authority, and Trust) framework, we will stick with RAU for now.

As SEO specialists, our role involves facilitating search engines to:

- Crawl and find our website/content easily.

- Index and comprehend the essence of our content.

- Rank our website to present it to users effectively.

By focusing on problem-solving, we create a successful SEO strategy that benefits both search engines and users.

Speaking of problem-solving, would you agree that the first step of solving a problem is identifying the problem?

And That is what keyword research is all about.

Keyword Research

I firmly believe that keyword research constitutes 50% of SEO. Without targeting the right keywords, your entire SEO effort would be futile - trust me, I have experienced that firsthand.

Now, let us delve into understanding what makes a keyword "right." Keywords, also known as search queries, are the words and phrases users input into search engines.

Focusing on relevancy, we can agree that understanding what users search for is essential to making your content relevant.

In this context, I would like to borrow a powerful definition from the legendary Peter Drucker about marketing:

"The aim of marketing is to know and understand the customer so well that the product or service fits them and sells itself."

Similarly, keyword research and SEO aim to comprehend what users seek, allowing you to create content or solutions that fit their needs seamlessly and naturally.

The essence of keyword research lies in discovering what people are searching for and gauging the demand for those queries.

However, not all keywords are created equal. You must grasp the distinction between head and tail keywords and, more importantly, understand the intent behind each keyword.

To conduct effective keyword research, follow these steps:

- Begin with a broad "seed keyword."
- Use tools like Ahrefs keyword generator and Alsoasked to expand your keyword list.
- Google your seed keyword and explore related queries and auto-complete suggestions.
- Cluster the gathered keywords into primary, secondary, and related categories.
- Repeat these steps to create multiple keyword clusters, aiming for at least 10-15 keywords in each.

However, your work is not complete yet.

Assessing supply - that is, the number of websites targeting the same keywords - is vital to understanding your competition.

To do this, use the following search operator on Google with your primary keyword: "allintitle:primary keyword."

For instance, if your primary keyword is "why are my tomato plants turning yellow," search for "allintitle:why are my tomato plants turning yellow" in Google.

This will reveal the number of results for that query, indicating how many websites or pages are targeting the same keyword.

Remember, keyword selection is not solely about search volume; it also involves considering the competition. Analysing both demand and supply will help you make informed decisions while selecting the keywords to target.

OnPage SEO

Achieving high rankings in search results is undeniably challenging. With numerous ranking factors at play, there is only so much you can do. However, some elements on your web pages lie within your control.

By optimizing these elements, you can ensure your pages provide users with a rich and unique experience.

Welcome to the world of OnPage SEO - a way to optimize your pages and increase their relevance for the chosen keywords, aiding search engines in understanding and organizing your content.

As you may recall from the R-A-U framework, the first step is Relevancy, and OnPage SEO centers around precisely that.

The objective of OnPage SEO is to make your page as relevant as possible to the search query (keyword). According to Google, the search giant itself acknowledges the importance of relevance in its ranking criteria.

So, how do you achieve increased relevance for your pages? Pay attention to these crucial on-page elements:

- **Title Tag:** The HTML attribute specifying the main headline of your webpage, displayed in search results. Aim for a catchy headline around 50-60 characters or 580 pixels, incorporating your primary keyword while still appealing to users.

- **Meta Description:** The HTML attribute providing a brief summary of your webpage below the link in search results. Keep it under 160 characters, prioritize the user-first approach, and naturally include the primary keyword.

- **URL:** This is the link of your page, and you have control over how it appears. Use your primary keyword in the URL, making it short, avoiding stop words, using hyphens instead of underscores, and eliminating spaces.

- **Header Tags:** HTML attributes that differentiate headings and subheadings, creating a well-structured content hierarchy. H1 refers to the main heading, usually the post title. Include the primary keyword naturally in the H1 tag and use other secondary and LSI keywords in H2-H6 tags.

- **Images:** Break up the text monotony with appealing images, which also offer more space to include keywords. Optimize images by using keyword-rich file names and alt tags (descriptive text for images) for user accessibility and attracting traffic.

- **Content:** The heart of OnPage SEO - content is vital. Write content centered around your keywords, then optimize all major elements for OnPage SEO. Sprinkle your keywords contextually and naturally throughout the content, answering users' queries and providing valuable information.

Remember, OnPage SEO places the power in your hands. Focus on what you can control first, creating a rich user experience and aiding search engines in finding relevant responses to queries. These efforts will contribute significantly to your SEO success.

Technical SEO

Technical SEO plays a critical role in enhancing your website's crawlability, indexability, speed, and credibility, resulting in improved rankings and efficiency. In essence, it simplifies the process for search engines to discover, understand, organize, and rank your website.

Similar to OnPage SEO, technical SEO also relies on several levers to optimize your website effectively. Let us explore these elements:

- **Site Architecture:** Just like a city with poor infrastructure hampers traffic flow, a poorly constructed site architecture obstructs crawlers. Two recommended approaches are Siloed Architecture and Topic Clusters, both contributing to better crawlability.

- **Crawl Analysis and Optimisation:** Considering the vastness of the internet, Google's search engine crawlers allocate time efficiently based on your site's crawl budget. By understanding your website's crawlability, as indicated in the Google Search Console coverage report, you can optimize the process using the robots.txt file.

- **Sitemaps:** An XML sitemap serves as a table of contents for your website, aiding in discovering and updating pages. Using plugins like Rank Math or Yoast can automatically generate sitemaps, but remember to add them to the search console. Internal linking is also crucial for helping crawlers find content faster and improving indexing.

- **Schema Markup/Structured Data:** Employing structured data, also known as schema markup, enables search engines to crawl, organize, and display your content more effectively. It results in rich snippets in SERPs, improving CTR and indirectly influencing rankings.

- **Speed Optimisation:** Nobody enjoys a slow website, and this includes search engines. Ensuring a fast-loading website enhances user experience and boosts crawl rates. Google Pagespeed Insights can help benchmark and optimize your site, considering core web vitals like Largest Contentful Paint (LCP), First Input Delay (FID), and Cumulative Layout Shift (CLS), among others.

To achieve a speedy website, consider the following steps:

- o Choose a reliable hosting company.
- o Use a Content Distribution Network (CDN) or Cloudflare.
- o Opt for a fast theme.
- o Utilize appropriate plugins, such as WP Rocket.

By focusing on technical SEO, you enhance your website's overall performance, making it more appealing to both users and search engines. A well-optimized website increases the likelihood of higher rankings and improved visibility, ultimately contributing to your online success.

Off-Page SEO

Let us delve into the fascinating world of Off-Page SEO. This aspect involves external actions taken to enhance your website's authority, with backlinks playing a significant role in the process.

So, what exactly is a backlink?

It is a hyperlink from one website to another. When website B receives a link from website A, it becomes a backlink.

Now, why are backlinks so crucial? To understand this, let us go back in time to when Google revolutionized search engines with the PageRank algorithm.

This ingenious concept, named after Larry Page, assigned a web page a quality score or PageRank (PR) ranging from 0 to 10.

Pages with more links pointing to them had a higher PageRank, implying greater authority.

Today, backlinks still reign as one of the most crucial ranking factors. They serve as votes of authority and credibility, affecting search engine rankings.

Link juice is the authority passed from one website to another through links, and the quality of backlinks determines the authority it carries.

To maintain a diverse and healthy backlink profile, consider these factors:

- Backlinks from unique root domains
- Backlinks from high-authority websites
- Relevance to your website
- A balance between dofollow and nofollow links
- Anchor text diversity

While it is ideal to earn backlinks through valuable content creation, you can also create, buy, or even make them using Private Blog Networks (PBNs). However, buying links comes with risks and requires caution.

Building backlinks through ethical and strategic means can significantly enhance your website's authority, visibility, and, ultimately, its success in search engine rankings.

Always prioritize value-driven content and organic link-building to ensure a strong foundation for Off-Page SEO endeavours.

Local SEO

Local SEO is a powerful strategy that focuses on optimizing your online presence to attract real-world customers.

Particularly beneficial for brick-and-mortar businesses that rely on physical foot traffic or online visibility to connect with customers offline, Local SEO holds a geographical component that sets it apart from traditional SEO.

In Local SEO, search queries often include city names (e.g., Chinese restaurants in Bangalore) or a "near me" element (e.g., petrol bunk near me).

These queries frequently trigger the appearance of a "map pack" on search results, showing local businesses relevant to the user's location. Alongside the map pack, there are the usual 10 organic results.

You might wonder if Local SEO applies to businesses without physical stores. The answer is a resounding yes.

Even exclusively online businesses can benefit from a Google Business Profile, which offers an excellent platform for collecting reviews and engaging with customers.

To ensure high rankings in Local SEO, several factors come into play, such as a complete and optimized Google Business Profile, primary and secondary categories, consistent and accurate citations, citations from authoritative websites, website authority, backlink profile, location name in On-Page elements, reviews, ratings, distance from the city center, and distance from searchers.

However, among these factors, none are as crucial as having a complete and optimized Google Business Profile. Setting up this profile is straightforward and only requires a Google/Gmail account.

Once established, you can manage and modify your business information without going through a review process if your profile is verified.

Another essential aspect of Local SEO is citations, which are essentially the backlinks of the local search world.

A citation includes the name, address, and phone number (NAP) of a local business mentioned online, with or without a link to the website.

Any website that references your business's NAP is considered a citation.

By understanding and leveraging these Local SEO principles, you can improve your online visibility, attract local customers, and enhance your business's success in the real world.

So do not overlook the potential of Local SEO, as it can provide significant benefits with manageable effort.

This content was contributed by Sanjay Shenoy, and I really appreciate his work in the field of SEO.

Let us now explore how SEO can be leveraged across the full A3R3 funnel.

SEO across the A3R3 Funnel

Awareness Stage

- **Objective:** Attract potential customers' attention and make them aware of your brand.

- **Keyword Research:** Identify relevant keywords related to your industry, products, or services. For instance, a SaaS company might target keywords like "best project management software."

- **Content Creation:** Develop high-quality, informative content such as blog posts, infographics, or videos that answer common questions in your industry. An example could be a skincare brand creating a blog post about "10 Tips for Glowing Skin."

Acquisition Stage

- **Objective:** Capture the interest of potential customers and encourage them to engage with your brand.

- **On-Page SEO:** Optimize landing pages with relevant keywords, compelling meta descriptions, and clear calls-to-action. An online course platform might optimize a landing page for "Learn Digital Marketing Online."

- **Local SEO:** If relevant, optimize your business for local searches. For example, a café might optimize for "best coffee shop in [city name]."

Activation Stage

- **Objective:** Encourage users to take specific actions that indicate their interest and intent to engage further.

- **Engaging Content:** Provide valuable resources, like eBooks, webinars, or free trials. A software company could offer a free trial for their project management tool.

- **User Experience:** Ensure your website is user-friendly and responsive on all devices. A travel agency might focus on responsive design for their vacation booking platform.

Revenue Stage

- **Objective:** Convince potential customers to make a purchase or subscribe to your services.

- **Product Pages Optimization:** Make sure product/service pages are well-optimized for both users and search engines. An e-commerce store could optimize a product page for "women's running shoes."

- **Rich Snippets:** Implement structured data to display additional information in search results, like prices or ratings. A review website might use rich snippets to show star ratings for their listed products.

Retention Stage

- **Objective:** Keep existing customers engaged and encourage repeat interactions.

- **Regular Blog Updates:** Publish new and relevant content consistently to keep users returning. A recipe website could post weekly recipe ideas.

- **Email Newsletter:** Use optimized content in your email newsletters to keep your subscribers informed and engaged. An online magazine might send out a weekly newsletter featuring the latest articles.

Referral Stage:

- **Objective:** Encourage satisfied customers to refer others to your brand.

- **User-Generated Content:** Encourage customers to leave reviews and share their experiences. A fitness app might feature success stories from users on their website.

- **Social Sharing:** Make your content easily shareable across social media platforms. An interior design platform could create visually appealing infographics for users to share on Pinterest.

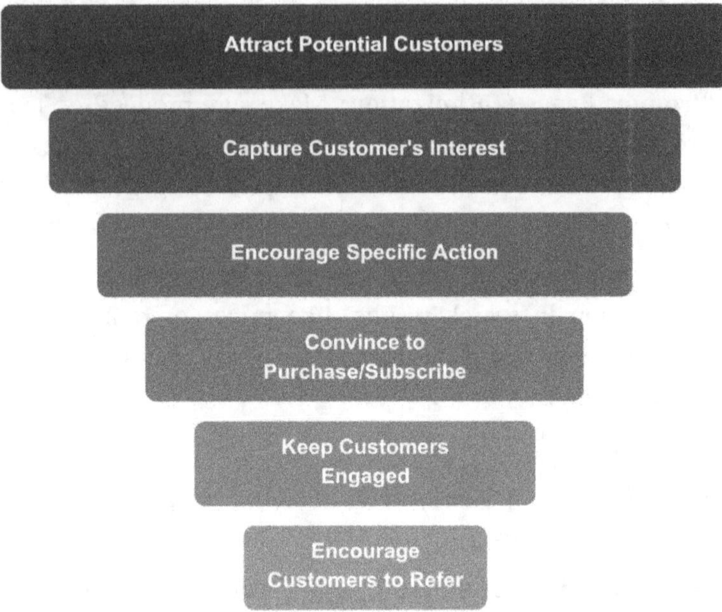

Remember, the key to successful SEO across the A3R3 funnel is relevance, quality, and consistency.

Align your SEO strategies with the user's intent at each stage to provide value and support their journey.

Tools for SEO

With so many SEO tools, it can become daunting to pick the right tools.

For my agency, we use a combination of ChatGPT, Copy.AI, SEMrush and Google Search Console for most of our clients.

Let us start with the 5 fundamental tools:

Google Search Console

- **Use:** Monitoring website performance and indexing status on Google.
- **Potential Uses:** Track keyword rankings, analyse click-through rates, and detect indexing issues.

Ahrefs

- **Use:** Comprehensive backlink analysis and keyword research.
- **Potential Uses:** Identify competitor backlinks, track your site's backlink profile, and find keyword opportunities.

SEMrush

- **Use:** All-in-one SEO suite for keyword research, site audits, and competitor analysis.
- **Potential Uses:** Identify high-performing keywords, analyse competitors' strategies, and track ranking changes.

Moz Pro

- **Use:** Offers site audits, keyword research, and link analysis.
- **Potential Uses:** Identify and fix technical SEO issues, research keywords, and track your site's domain authority.

Yoast SEO

- **Use:** WordPress plugin for optimizing on-page content.
- **Potential Uses:** Analyse content for SEO, generate XML sitemaps, and control breadcrumbs and metadata.

Next, let us look at 5 AI tools to give you an edge.

MarketMuse

- **Use:** Content optimization and keyword research using AI-driven analysis.
- **Potential Uses:** Generate content briefs, identify topic gaps, and improve on-page SEO.

BrightEdge

- **Use:** AI-powered platform for SEO recommendations and competitive insights.
- **Potential Uses:** Monitor keyword performance, track SERP rankings, and gain insights into competitor strategies.

Serpstat

- **Use:** AI-based SEO and PPC research tools.

- **Potential Uses:** Analyse backlinks, track keyword rankings, and conduct site audits for technical improvements.

CopyAI

- **Use:** AI-powered content generation tool.
- **Potential Uses:** Generate high-quality SEO-focused content, meta descriptions, and title tags.

Jasper

- **Use:** AI-driven platform for SEO optimization and content creation.
- **Potential Uses:** Create optimized content, improve keyword targeting, and analyse SEO performance.

Chapter 27

Sales Hacking for Growth

Contributing Author: Jayant Padhi

Bio: Jayant Kumar is a seasoned consultant at PixelTrack with a unique blend of data-driven tactics and creative strategy. Over the years, he has been helping digital service providers streamline their operations, facilitating 30-40 booked meetings through an effective system of lead acquisition and trust building. His commitment to his clients extends to sales, where he helps set up lead generation systems and provides sales training.

His achievements are notable, with significant contributions to various organizations. For instance, he and his team launched the YourStory Start-Up Course generating over 1 Crore + in revenue, and increased Amaari Parfum's Sales by 792%. At PixelTrack, he personally generated over $1M in revenue by mid-2023.

In 2012, Brett Adcock embarked on a journey to revolutionize the recruiting market.

He founded Vettery with a vision to take the industry online, leveraging machine learning and a two-sided marketplace to facilitate interviews at scale.

The only hurdle was a behemoth competitor, Hired.com, armed with 15x more capital, a workforce 10x larger, and a two-year head start.

Hired.com had a well-recognized brand, a robust team, and impressive funding of $150M.

Based in San Francisco, they were geared to dominate the online recruitment industry.

However, their seemingly unbeatable strength would ironically lead to their undoing.

The battleground was the two-sided recruiting marketplace, where both Vettery and Hired had to attract employers and candidates alike.

The goal was simple: to grow the marketplace.

The more qualified employers and candidates, the faster the growth.

However, Hired's growth primarily relied on costly paid ads, which was not a viable strategy for Vettery due to their limited budget.

Given their financial constraints, Vettery had to think outside the box.

They devised three tactics:

- Guerrilla Marketing,
- Outbound Lead-Gen Marketing, and
- Outbound Sales via Sales Development Representatives (SDRs).

Now instead of randomly cold calling strangers and asking them for money, Vettery did something different.

They would physically mail out a drone helicopter with a note to call them back for the free remote control.

Everyone was calling for this!

In one year, Vettery shipped over 20,000 helicopters.

Their Outbound Lead-Gen Marketing strategy involved a team of marketers who emailed potential clients, generating leads with double-digit response rates.

Simultaneously, SDRs focused on cold calling and messaging, resulting in over 100 calls per day per rep.

These innovative approaches drastically reduced Vettery's acquisition costs, allowing them to offer a cheaper service and making them less reliant on external capital.

In contrast, Hired followed the traditional Silicon Valley model—raising and spending enormous capital in pursuit of customer acquisition.

Two structure advantages emerged due to this:

1. Vettery's service was cheaper. Vettery did not have any overheads. They had unlimited hiring subscriptions which increased demand. Plus, it was more lucrative for the recruiters.

2. Vettery was less dependent on outside capital. 15X less capital raised. They did not have to convince any Venture Capitalist.

Meanwhile, Hired was playing a different game.

Hired was running the traditional silicon valley playbook:

Raise a lot of money and spend it at any cost to acquire customers. The consensus was that, you do that enough, and you win.

Brett Adcock, the founder deliberately stayed away from this strategy, knowing that it was not sustainable.

Then Covid happened.

Vettery was able to weather the storm and grow sustainably.

Meanwhile, Hired ended up running out of capital during Covid as companies slowed hiring down.

In 2021, Vettery acquired Hired and changed their name to Hired.

They took over the brand name and their identity, demonstrating that success is not just about money.

It is about discipline, creativity, grit, and playing the long game.

Although it looks like a classic David and Goliath story, there is a lot to learn from this story about sales hacking.

As a business owner trying to build something cool and sell it to the world, faces the challenge of selling at some point.

But when every single one of your competitor's messages is screaming, "Buy my stuff," you need to stand out like, "Here is something for you."

Do not worry. You do not have to buy thousands of drones for it.

In this chapter I will use some tactics I have used in my career to book appointments through an optimized outreach process that has proven to work for over 130+ businesses.

What is Outreach, and How does it work?

Well, the approach is simple.

There is a business you want to work with. But they do not know you yet. Now, all you have to do is reach out to them and start a conversation.

That's it. Not so difficult, right?

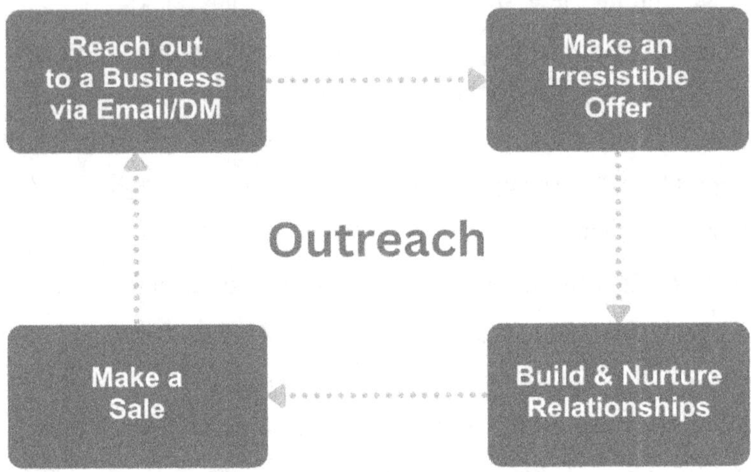

Essentially outreach is when you email or DM someone you do not know, hoping to get a response.

It is a bit like going up to a girl (or boy) you like at a party and starting a conversation, except you are doing it over email.

The goal of cold outreach is to build a relationship with the person you are outreaching, hoping that they will eventually do business with you.

Read that again...The goal is to build a relationship first.

However, do not go too far here.

If done incorrectly, you will become a spammer and quickly get your emails ignored or deleted.

You do not want to approach a girl at a party and ask for her hand in marriage.

Similarly, never ask for work right on your first email.

Remember, they do not know you yet.

The best way is to start forming a friendship.

So how do you approach someone without being a total creep?

The key is to personalize your emails as much as possible.

And here is how you do it.

Start by finding out who your target contact is and then doing some research on them.

Find out what their interests are, where they work, what their job title is, etc.

The more the better.

The more you know about them, the easier it will be to write a personalized email that piques their interest.

Find something you really appreciate about them or their business.

And highlight that in your email.

Here is my framework for any kind of cold outreach.

Here is how it goes:

Subject: It starts with an intriguing subject line that makes them open your email.

No need to be formal.

You are sending to people, not robots.

For this context, I am using examples of cold emails I send. You can use a similar structure for any kind of platform.

Here are a few examples:

- Recorded this for you Rishabh
- This might help
- Writing a book?

Complement: Complement something you like in your prospect's social profile or website.

This builds rapport with the prospect you want to talk to.

Here is an example:

- "I attended the launch of the ABC product. Absolutely mind blown by the fact that it can do XYZ."

Value: Here you pretty much try to add value to your prospect. This is your version of the drone that the founder of your target company wants.

Although it is not guerilla marketing, it helps immensely when it comes to cold outreach.

It goes something like this:

- "I know you are busy amping up {company name} to new heights. I have a couple of ideas to help you boost ROI on your email & WhatsApp Campaigns.
- I have recorded a quick 2 min video for you."

Why does this work?

It is non-intrusive.

It delivers value (in the form of a video) without asking for anything in return.

CTA: Next, add a specific call to action for them to take by reading your email.

This is to get them interested in the stuff you are sending them. This is the coffee date I was talking about.

- Example: "Should I send it over?"

Do not over complicate it.

Overall, the email looks like the following:

And it gets responses like this:

Hi Abhishek,
Must say I was very impressed with your "pick-up line" - as it definitely got me interested to write back to you!
Yes please do share your ideas - I would love to hear them out and explore what is possible.
Thanks and Stay Well -

Tel:
Web:
Facebook:

On Thu, Jun 29, 2023 at 4:07 PM , wrote:

Hey — Loved your packaging, my first impression was "is that the founder picture" but when I scrolled down and realized "Damn", correct me if I'm wrong but are these farmer's pictures on your products?

I know you're busy amping up to new heights.

I've a couple of ideas to help you boost ROI on your email & WhatsApp Campaigns.

Once they show interest you try to send the resource and ask for a call-in return.

But is this Scalable?

Now this method seems tedious and a lot of clients I meet say, "Jayant, this doesn't seem so scalable."

The way most people think scaling is wrong.

When I asked even my colleagues, their definition of scaling up is doing more work.

Which is true but not in all cases.

When it comes to FB ads, you add more creatives, put more ad budgets, and you scale up.

When it comes to YouTube, you hire a video team and pump up the number of videos you produce.

The reality is, scaling up is essentially the outcome that gets multiplied by the multiplication of capital, effort, or time.

Now people misunderstand how cold outreach scaling works.

When you want to scale cold outreach, you do not necessarily send more cold emails.

Instead, you increase the precision.

And target people in a very narrow segment facing a very specific problem.

This increases the chances of replies and booked meetings.

Now you might argue, the amount of effort increases.

Sure, it does.

The result also increases dramatically. Infact, according to Will Atrock, founder of <u>Lavender AI,</u> personalized emails with value receive as much as 1200% more response rates than generic emails.

Let us compare.

Generic "So called scalable" Message	Specific Message with Value
Sent 1000 emails	Sent 300 emails
0.5-1% Reply rate	Up to 10% reply rate (sometimes up to 20 if it is relevant)
10 Booked Meetings	30 Booked meetings

The bottom line is that, in order to get your customer's attention, you have to be specific, lead with value and simplify your call to actions.

Crafting an Irresistible Offer

Now that you have captured your audience's attention, it is time to present them with an offer they simply cannot refuse.

By putting yourself in your customer's shoes, you can tailor your offer to meet their needs and provide them with a valuable solution.

Here are the key elements to consider when crafting your offer:

Each answers a specific question in your audience's mind

- Solution: "What problem are you solving?"

- Price: "How much does it cost?"
- Bonuses: "What more do I get from this?"
- Guarantees: "What if it doesn't work?"

Remember, your offer is essentially a bridge that connects your product or service to your customers' needs.

A well-built bridge will seamlessly guide your customers towards a solution, building trust and confidence along the way.

To ensure your offer is sturdy and inviting, focus on thoroughly understanding your target audience, addressing their pain points, and providing a clear path to the desired outcome.

By considering each element of your offer and how it resonates with your customers, you can create an irresistible offer that is hard to resist.

Solution: "What problem are you solving?"

Every great offer starts with a clear understanding of the problem you are solving.

Your customers are facing challenges, and they are looking for solutions.

So, your product is not just a product; it is a key that can unlock a door blocking their path.

However, remember that your customers may not view their challenges in the same way you do.

They need to perceive your product as the best fit for their needs.

So, take the time to understand their perspective, their pain points, and their desired outcomes.

For instance, suppose you are selling a project management software.

Your customers' problem is not a lack of software; it is the chaos and inefficiency in managing projects.

Your software is a solution because it brings order and boosts productivity.

Price: "How much does it cost?"

The price of your product is more than a number.

It is a value statement.

Your customers are asking, "Is this product worth this amount?"

To answer this question convincingly, you need to demonstrate the value they will get in return for their investment.

Break it down into tangible benefits.

For example, if your project management software can save a company 10 hours a week, quantify that in dollar terms based on the average hourly rate of the employees.

Bonuses: "What more do I get from this?"

Bonuses are like cherries on top of your offer.

They add extra value and can tip the scales in your favour when customers are comparing you to your competitors.

However, ensure your bonuses complement the main offer and contribute to solving the customer's problem.

For instance, if you are selling workout supplements, you might offer a free diet and exercise plan tailored to the customer's fitness goals.

This shows your commitment to their overall wellbeing, not just selling supplements.

Guarantees: "What if it doesn't work?"

No matter how compelling your offer is, prospective customers will always have doubts and objections.

This is where guarantees come into play.

By removing the risk associated with the purchase, you build trust and make it easier for the customer to say yes.

A 30-day money-back guarantee, for example, shows you stand by the effectiveness of your product.

You are basically telling customers, "Hey, if it doesn't work for you, no problem.

You can have your money back."

Finally, remember that crafting an irresistible offer is not about deception or manipulation.

It is about truthfully presenting your product in a way that resonates with your customers.

It is about showing them that you understand their problems, and you are here to help.

It is about building that sturdy, inviting bridge that leads them to a solution.

And when you do this right, your offer becomes truly irresistible.

Building and Nurturing Relationships

Alright, you have made your killer offer.

Now it is time to build and nurture relationships with your prospects.

But how? It is all about personalization.

People want to feel special, not like they are just another name on your list.

The first step in building a relationship with your prospects is understanding them.

Every person is different, with their own unique set of needs, wants, and pain points.

When you understand these individual differences, you can tailor your communication and offers accordingly.

The Very First Interaction

For example, when a prospect downloads a free eBook from your website or requests the data you sent in the first email, it is an opportunity to learn about their interests.

You can then send a personalized thank you email, acknowledging their interest, and suggesting additional resources that might be helpful to them.

Engage with your prospects on Social Media

Participate in the conversations they are having, comment on their posts, share their content, and respond to their queries.

This kind of interaction shows that you are interested in them and not just in selling your product.

Nurturing Relationships

Building a relationship is just the beginning.

To turn prospects into loyal customers, you must nurture these relationships over time. Here, consistency is key.

Regularly touch base with your prospects, offer them valuable content, and provide solutions to their problems.

A key tool in nurturing relationships is your CRM system.

With a CRM, you can track each prospect's journey, from the first point of contact to the final sale.

This helps you understand their behaviour, identify opportunities for engagement, and personalize your communication.

For instance, if a prospect visits your pricing page but does not make a purchase, it could indicate they are interested but have some reservations.

A personalized email offering to answer any questions they might have can make a big difference.

Follow-ups and Demos

Follow-ups and product demos are vital in the sales process.

But how you conduct them can make or break the deal.

Tailoring your demos to address the specific needs of your prospects can drastically increase your conversion rates.

After a demo, follow up with a personalized email summarizing the key points covered, addressing any concerns they raised, and inviting them to take the next step.

Remember, this is not a one-size-fits-all email.

Each prospect is unique, and your follow-up should reflect that.

Continuous Value Addition

Value addition should not stop after a sale.

To turn customers into brand advocates, you need to continually offer them value.

Regularly share relevant content, provide exclusive offers, and invite them to events. Ask for their feedback and show them that their opinion matters.

Remember, building and nurturing relationships is a long-term game.

It takes time, patience, and consistent effort.

But the payoff is well worth it. When you have strong relationships with your customers, they not only become loyal buyers, but also powerful advocates for your brand.

In the long run, this can significantly reduce your customer acquisition costs and increase your overall profitability.

So, keep reaching out, keep offering value, and keep nurturing those relationships. Because in sales, relationships are everything.

Growth Hacking for Sales

Now Let us dive into some growth hacking techniques for sales.

Growth hacking - a term that often reverberates within the realms of startups and digital businesses.

It is all about out-of-the-box, creative tactics that can trigger exponential growth with minimal resources.

For us, salespeople, it is about weaving together marketing techniques, data insights, and technology to propel sales growth.

Let us delve into some examples to help you gain a clearer understanding.

Let us begin with a story that many of us know - Dropbox.

This file hosting service leveraged a simple but ingenious growth hack: a referral program.

Dropbox offered extra storage space to users who referred others to the service. The result?

Their users, enticed by the prospect of more space, turned into a powerful, voluntary sales force that drove new sign-ups.

Their user base skyrocketed from 100,000 to 4 million in just over a year, demonstrating the power of turning your customers into your promoters.

Another compelling example is the Dollar Shave Club. This company managed to create a tidal wave in the online market with a humorous, low-budget video.

In the video, the founder walks around a warehouse, wittily demonstrating the value proposition of their razor subscription service.

The video went viral and resulted in 12,000 sign-ups within the first 48 hours.

Not only did this campaign bring attention to their product, but it also helped establish their brand personality, proving that creativity can indeed lead to explosive growth.

While these examples are from big names, growth hacking is not exclusive to large-scale businesses.

Even small and medium businesses can utilize these strategies for substantial growth.

Consider the strategy of creating valuable, shareable content that positions your brand as a thought leader in your industry.

By offering insightful blog posts, eBooks, or webinars, you attract prospective customers who are looking for expert advice.

When your content offers them the needed solution, they are more likely to consider your product or service.

Another technique is leveraging social proof to build trust and credibility.

Testimonials, case studies, or customer reviews can serve as powerful tools to convince potential customers.

Seeing others benefit from your product can often nudge a prospect from considering purchasing.

Finally, remember to embrace technology in your growth hacking efforts.

From automating your follow-up emails to analysing user behaviour with CRM systems, technology can significantly enhance your sales process.

It allows you to serve more customers more efficiently and provides insights to continuously improve your strategies.

In essence, growth hacking for sales is about thinking creatively, testing new strategies, and leveraging data and technology to optimize performance.

It is about not being content with traditional methods and having the audacity to disrupt the norm.

In the words of Robert Frost, taking the road less travelled can make all the difference.

So, stay curious, stay creative, and keep hacking your way to exponential sales growth!

The above chapter was contributed by Jayant Padhi.

PART 4: EVOLUTION

Chapter 28

Design Growth Workflows that Scale

I have worked with over 50+ clients and seen over 1000+ workflows.

One key success factor for most high-growth startups is finding just a few growth workflows that can scale. It is easy to see short-lived success from growth hacking.

But to really achieve long-term growth, putting the growth marketing process in place to find scalable workflows is the key.

In this chapter, we will learn how to design growth workflows.

Examples of Workflows

Let us start with a few simple examples of workflows that will help you visualize what I mean when I use the word workflows.

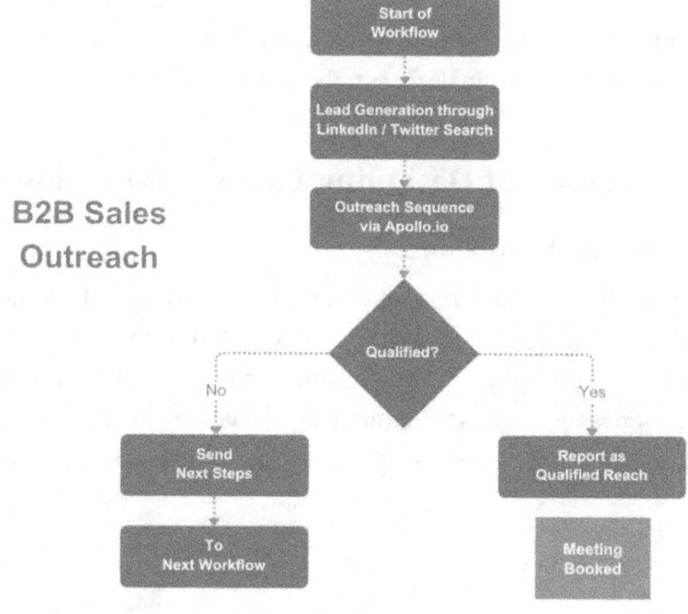

Now, let us look at another example of workflow for a local small
business.

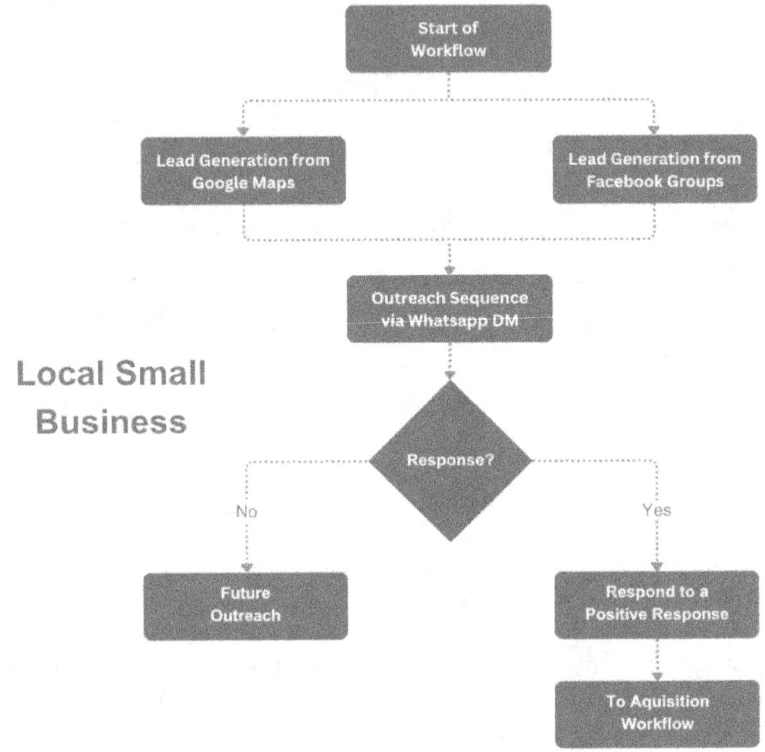

As you can see in the above examples, workflows show the step-by-step
process, and the decision-making involved in the process.

3 Key Principles of Designing Growth Workflows

Data-Driven Decision-Making

Growth workflows should rely on data and analytics to drive decision-
making. By collecting, analysing, and interpreting relevant data,
businesses can gain insights into customer behaviour, market trends, and
the effectiveness of growth strategies. Data-driven decision-making
ensures that actions are based on evidence rather than assumptions.

Iterative Experimentation

Growth workflows should embrace an iterative and experimental approach.

By continuously testing and iterating on strategies, companies can learn from successes and failures, refine their approaches, and optimize their growth efforts. Iterative experimentation allows for agility and adaptation in a dynamic market environment.

Interlinking Workflows and Building a Growth Machine

Once you have designed your growth workflows, you can interlink them to create something I call the "growth machine."

This growth machine can continue to work for you like an engine and is scalable in the long run.

You may need to tighten a few screws from time to time and replace parts (think of this as replacing channels or finding new ones), but overall, you will have a growing machine.

5 Key elements of a growth workflow

1. **Goal Setting:** Keep your OMTM in mind for each workflow being designed

2. **Mapping the Customer Journey:** Identify which stage of the A3R3 funnel the workflow is designed for.

3. **Data Collection and Analysis:** Establish mechanisms for collecting relevant data through the workflow and measure the key metrics from each workflow/

4. **Experimentation and Iteration:** Incorporate a culture of experimentation and iteration into the workflow. You can scale the workflow only once you have tested alternatives and found the best performing version of the workflow.

5. **Cross-Functional Collaboration:** Foster collaboration and communication between different teams and departments involved in the growth workflow. I like to have a central

document with all workflows and it is shared with all my company teams.

Growth Workflows from Popular startups

Growth Workflow: User Onboarding

Startup: Slack

Focus Stage (A3R3 funnel): Activation

Workflow:

- Initial when a user signs up for Slack.
- User receives a welcome email with a link to download the Slack app.
- User installs the Slack app on their device.
- User is prompted to create a team or join an existing one.
- User completes a guided tour of Slack's main features.
- User is encouraged to invite team members to join the Slack workspace.
- User receives regular email updates about new features and tips for using Slack effectively.
- User is prompted to integrate other tools and services into Slack.
- User is encouraged to participate in the Slack community and join relevant channels.
- User becomes an active and engaged member of the Slack platform.

Growth Workflow: Referral Program

Startup: Dropbox

Focus Stage: Referral

Workflow:

- User signs up for Dropbox and installs the Dropbox app on their device.

- User receives a welcome email inviting them to refer friends to join Dropbox.

- User is provided with a unique referral link to share with friends.

- User shares the referral link via email, social media, or other communication channels.

- Referred friends receive an invitation to join Dropbox and are incentivized with additional storage space.

- Referred friends sign up for Dropbox using the referral link.

- The referring user receives additional storage space as a reward for successful referrals.

- Referring user is encouraged to continue referring more friends.

- Referred friends are also encouraged to refer others, creating a viral loop of growth.

- Dropbox expands its user base through successful referrals and incentivized sharing.

In the next example, let us look at a longer workflow that covers all 3 stages of Awareness, Acquisition, and Activation.

Growth Workflow: Content Marketing

Startup: HubSpot

Stages: Awareness, Acquisition, and Activation

Workflow:

- HubSpot creates high-quality blog posts, e-books, and other valuable content related to inbound marketing.

- Content is published on the HubSpot blog and promoted through social media channels.

- Interested readers are encouraged to subscribe to the HubSpot newsletter for regular updates.

- Subscribers receive email newsletters with curated content, tips, and insights.

- HubSpot offers free webinars and downloadable resources to educate and engage subscribers.

- Subscribers are encouraged to sign up for HubSpot's free trial or request a demo of their marketing software.

- Trial users receive personalized onboarding and support to help them get started with HubSpot's tools.

- Trial users are nurtured through email sequences and in-app messaging to drive activation and product adoption.

- Users are provided with educational resources, case studies, and success stories to maximize their value from HubSpot.

- Users become advocates for HubSpot, referring others and contributing to the growth of the company.

In the case of Hubspot, you can see that it can be further broken down into mini-workflows for each stage of the funnel.

However, it can be treated as a single workflow for the content marketing team as they can track the entire user journey.

These are just a few examples of growth workflows implemented by successful startups.

Each workflow is tailored to the specific goals and target audience of the startup, and the steps are refined over time based on data and feedback.

The key is to identify the most effective channels and tactics to drive growth, continuously optimize the workflow, and scale the processes to achieve sustainable growth.

We are now getting into slightly more complex examples below as I will show you how startups can create workflows across the A3R3 funnel.

Let us look at the example of Glossier below:

Growth Workflow: Influencer Partnership

Startup: Glossier

Workflow:

- Glossier identifies relevant influencers in the beauty and skincare industry. (Awareness)

- Glossier reaches out to influencers via email or direct messages to introduce their brand and products. (Acquisition)

- Influencers receive complimentary Glossier products to try and review. (Activation)

- Influencers create and share honest reviews and tutorials featuring Glossier products on their social media platforms and blogs. (Activation)

- Influencers provide unique discount codes to their followers, incentivizing them to make a purchase on the Glossier website. (Revenue)

- Glossier tracks the performance of each influencer's promotion using custom referral codes or affiliate links. (Referral)

- Glossier nurtures relationships with successful influencers, continuing to provide them with new products and exclusive offers. (Retention)

- Glossier's brand awareness and customer base expand through influencer collaborations and word-of-mouth referrals. (Referral)

Growth Workflow: Community Engagement

Startup: Patreon

Workflow:

- Patreon creates a dedicated online community platform where creators and patrons can interact. (Activation)

- Creators are encouraged to engage with their patrons through exclusive content, live Q&A sessions, and behind-the-scenes updates. (Retention)

- Patrons receive regular email newsletters highlighting new content and updates from their favourite creators. (Retention)

- Patreon hosts virtual events, such as webinars or workshops, where creators and patrons can connect and learn from each other. (Activation)

- Patrons are incentivized to upgrade to higher-tier membership levels to access additional perks and benefits. (Revenue)

- Patreon provides analytics and insights to creators, helping them understand their audience and optimize their offerings. (Retention)

- Creators and patrons are encouraged to invite friends and fellow creators to join the Patreon community. (Referral)

- Patreon continues to foster a supportive and engaged community, driving retention, and attracting new creators and patrons. (Retention)

Growth Workflow: Content Crowdsourcing

Startup: Canva

Workflow:

- Canva encourages users to create and share designs using their platform. (Activation)

- Users have the option to make their designs public and accessible to others for inspiration. (Awareness)

- Canva curates and features outstanding designs created by users on their social media channels and website. (Awareness)

- Canva holds design contests or challenges, inviting users to submit their best work for a chance to be featured or win prizes. (Activation)

- Canva encourages users to share their designs on social media using branded hashtags. (Awareness)

- Canva provides templates and design resources that users can customize and share with their own audiences, spreading awareness of the platform. (Awareness)

- Canva implements a referral program, offering rewards to users who refer others to sign up and use the platform. (Referral)

- Canva maintains an active blog and knowledge base, providing tutorials, tips, and design inspiration to engage and educate users. (Retention)

- Canva's user-generated content and community engagement contribute to brand awareness and attract new users to the platform. (Awareness)

These growth workflows demonstrate how lesser-known startups can leverage strategic tactics aligned with the A3R3 funnel stages to drive growth, engage their target audience, and build a scalable growth machine.

By tailoring workflows to their specific industry and target market, startups can establish a competitive advantage and foster sustainable growth.

Chapter 29

Amplify Growth with OPNs and OPAs

The best way to build an audience is to stand on the shoulders of giants.

The most common way of doing this is running ads where you are basically tapping into the audience of Meta or Google or other large channels.

However, a more cost-effective way of doing this is by leveraging smaller channels and their audiences and other people's networks.

There are 2 ways to do this:

OPNs (Other People's Networks) and **OPAs (Other People's Audiences)**

These concepts involve tapping into existing networks and audiences that have already been built by others, allowing businesses to leverage their influence, and credibility, and reach for their own growth.

What are OPNs?

OPNs refer to networks or communities that are already established, usually by other organizations in a particular niche or industry.

Here are some examples of popular startups, and their early user acquisition OPNs:

Startup	OPN
Airbnb	Craigslist, college campuses, homeowner associations
PayPal	eBay
Etsy	Craft fairs
Lyft	Startup offices
Dropbox	Hacker News (video)
Loom	ProductHunt
Tinder	College campuses

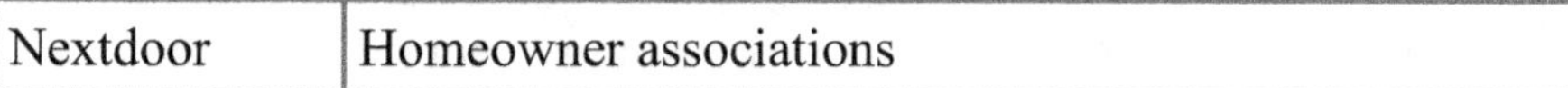

Nextdoor	Homeowner associations

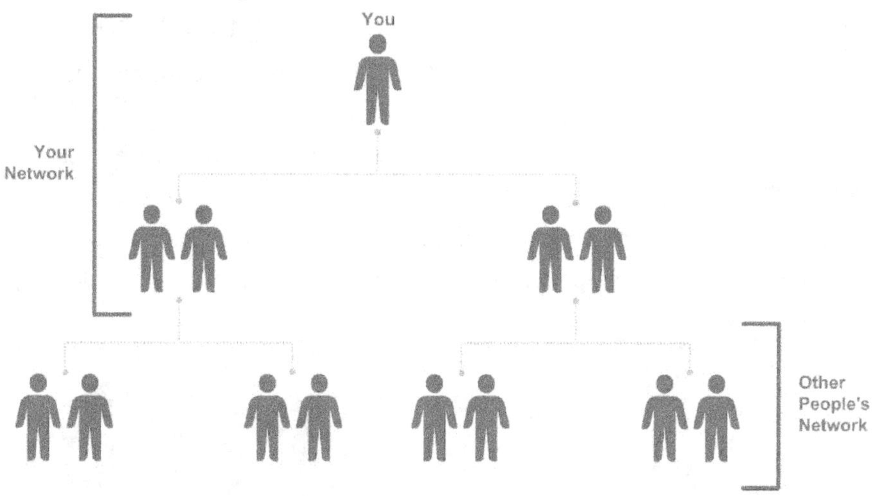

What are OPAs?

OPAs, on the other hand, are existing audiences that have been built and nurtured by individuals or organizations.

These can be emailing lists, social media followers, blog subscribers, or podcast listeners.

By collaborating with OPAs, businesses can leverage the existing audience to amplify their message, increase brand visibility, and attract new customers.

Here are some examples of OPAs:

OPAs	Example
Other people's podcasts	Guest appearances on popular podcasts
Other people's blogs	Guest blogging on established industry blogs
Other people's email list	Collaborative email campaigns with partner companies
Other people's events	Speaking engagements at industry conferences

Other people's webinars	Guest hosting webinars for partner organizations
Other people's ads	Sponsored content on influential websites
Other people's communities	Active participation in online communities and forums
Other people's LinkedIn posts	Collaborating on LinkedIn posts with industry influencers

I personally use all the above examples of OPAs for my own personal branding, as well as for promoting my agency, Mapplinks, and academy, GrowthGrad.

Why use OPNs and OPAs

Benefits and advantages of tapping into existing networks and audiences:

Speed and Efficiency

Partnering with OPNs and OPAs enables businesses to quickly access a large audience without the need to build their own network from scratch. This saves time and resources in audience acquisition and allows for faster growth.

Targeted and Relevant Connections

Collaborating with OPNs and OPAs that align with a business's target market ensures that their message reaches the right audience, increasing the chances of attracting qualified leads and customers.

Mutual Value Exchange

Effective collaborations with OPNs and OPAs are built on mutual benefit. By providing value to the network or audience, businesses can foster long-term relationships and establish themselves as trusted partners.

Increased Brand Visibility and Authority

Being featured or recommended by trusted OPNs and OPAs enhances a business's brand visibility, establishes them as an authority in their industry, and helps build trust with potential customers.

Expanded Reach

Collaborating with OPNs and OPAs allows businesses to extend their reach beyond their existing audience, exposing their brand and message to a wider pool of potential customers.

Targeted Exposure

By partnering with OPNs and OPAs that align with their target market, businesses can ensure that their message reaches an audience that is more likely to be interested in their products or services, resulting in higher quality leads.

Social Proof and Credibility

When a business is recommended or endorsed by a trusted OPN or featured to an established OPA, it lends credibility and social proof to the brand, making it more appealing to new customers.

Cost-Effective Growth

Leveraging OPNs and OPAs can be a cost-effective alternative to traditional marketing channels, as it allows businesses to tap into existing networks and audiences without the need for extensive advertising budgets.

3 Things to Look for in Potential OPAs and OPNs

I look for these 3 things while shortlisting potential OPAs and OPNs for me, or for my startup clients:

1. **Market Overlap:** Understand the target market and the overlap with your target audience.

2. **Engagement Analysis:** Evaluate the level of engagement within the identified networks.

3. **Alignment with Values and Goals:** Assess the alignment between the business's values, goals, and the values of the identified networks.

Once I have identified the list, I take it further and identify the way I can leverage the particular OPN / OPA.

Next, let us look at the different ways of leveraging OPNs and OPAs, once you have identified them.

Ways to Leverage OPNs and OPAs

To remember these methods, just remember the 3Ps framework we discussed earlier.

The 3Ps of Growth Hacking

P - Piggybacking

Piggybacking refers to leveraging existing networks and platforms to amplify your reach and gain visibility. It involves identifying established channels, communities, or platforms that align with your target audience and finding ways to tap into their existing audience base.

Examples of piggybacking include

- Guest blogging on popular industry blogs or publications to showcase your expertise and reach a wider readership.

- Participating in relevant online forums or communities where your target audience is active, providing valuable insights and building your brand presence.

- Engaging in social media conversations, sharing relevant content, and leveraging popular hashtags to increase visibility and attract new followers.

P - Partnerships

Partnerships involve collaborating with individuals, businesses, or organizations that have a complementary target audience or offer complementary products/services. By joining forces, you can expand your reach and leverage each other's strengths.

Examples of partnerships include:

- Co-creating content or hosting joint webinars with industry influencers or thought leaders to tap into their audience and gain credibility.

- Cross-promoting products/services with non-competing businesses through email newsletters or social media shoutouts to expose each other's offerings to new audiences.

- Collaborating with complementary startups or businesses to offer bundled packages or joint promotions that provide added value to customers and increase brand visibility.

P - Paid Opportunities

Paid opportunities involve investing resources to gain exposure and reach new audiences through advertising or sponsorship arrangements. While this requires financial investment, it can yield significant returns in terms of brand visibility and customer acquisition.

Examples of paid opportunities include:

- Sponsored content on influential blogs or media outlets that cater to your target audience, allowing you to tap into their readership and gain credibility.

- Paid advertising on smaller platforms, enabling you to target specific demographics and drive traffic to your website or landing pages.

- Collaborating with influencers or micro-influencers who have a significant following in your niche, paying them to promote your product or service to their engaged audience.

Partnering with complementary businesses for co-marketing campaigns, where you share the costs and benefits of promotional initiatives to reach a wider audience.

By leveraging piggybacking, partnerships, and paid opportunities, startups can strategically tap into existing networks, collaborate with key players in their industry, and invest in targeted promotions to amplify their growth and gain a competitive edge in the market.

Examples from Startups

Next, let us look at some examples of startups and how they leveraged specific OPNs and OPAs:

Startup	OPN/OPA Used	Method to Leverage OPN/OPA
Airbnb	Craigslist	Integrated Craigslist listings (Piggybacking)
PayPal	eBay	Provided payment services for eBay (Piggybacking)
Loom	Other people's blogs	Guest blogging on industry blogs
ProductHunt	Other people's events	Participating in industry events
Dropbox	Hacker News (video)	Sharing company updates on Hacker News

Tinder	College campuses	Targeted marketing campaigns on campuses
Lyft	Startup offices	On-site promotions and partnerships
Etsy	Craft fairs	Participating in local craft fairs
Nextdoor	Homeowner associations	Collaborating with associations for neighbourhood reach
Canva	Other people's podcasts	Guest appearances on popular podcasts
Buffer	Other people's blogs	Guest blogging on industry blogs
HubSpot	Other people's email list	Sponsored newsletter placements
Moz	Other people's webinars	Hosting webinars with industry experts
Slack	Other people's communities	Engaging in relevant online communities
Salesforce	Other people's ads	Display advertising on relevant websites
LinkedIn	Other people's LinkedIn posts	Engaging with influential LinkedIn posts
Shopify	Other people's communities	Partnering with online communities for brand exposure

Let us break down 3 of these examples in more detail:

Airbnb - Leveraging Craigslist

- **Startup:** Airbnb, an online marketplace for booking accommodations.

- **OPN Used:** Craigslist, a popular online classifieds platform.

- **Method:** Airbnb leveraged the existing user base and popularity of Craigslist by integrating Craigslist listings onto their platform. This allowed Airbnb to tap into Craigslist's vast user network and gain exposure to a large audience actively searching for accommodations.

- **P of the 3Ps:** Piggybacking.
- **Explanation:** By integrating Craigslist listings, Airbnb leveraged the reach and user engagement of Craigslist to attract potential users and property owners to their platform. This strategic partnership allowed Airbnb to accelerate its growth by leveraging the established user base and traffic of Craigslist.

PayPal - Collaborating with eBay

- **Startup:** PayPal, an online payments system.
- **OPN Used:** eBay, a leading online marketplace.
- **Method:** PayPal collaborated with eBay to provide payment services for eBay transactions. By offering a convenient and secure payment solution, PayPal became the preferred payment method for eBay users, which drove the adoption and usage of PayPal's services. This had started as piggybacking and eventually became a partnership.
- **P of the 3Ps:** Piggybacking (and then Partnership)
- **Explanation:** PayPal leveraged eBay's massive user base and established marketplace to position itself as the go-to payment solution. This integration provided a seamless payment experience for eBay users and enabled PayPal to gain widespread recognition and trust, leading to significant growth in its user base and transaction volume.

Loom - Guest Appearances on Podcasts

- **Startup:** Loom, a video messaging tool.
- **OPN Used:** Other people's podcasts.
- **Method:** Loom actively sought opportunities to appear as a guest on popular industry-related podcasts. They shared insights, tips, and use cases about their video messaging tool, demonstrating its value, and discussing its benefits to the audience.
- **P of the 3Ps:** Partnership

- **Explanation:** By leveraging other people's podcasts, Loom gained exposure to new and relevant audiences who were interested in topics related to video communication, remote work, and productivity. These podcast appearances allowed Loom to establish thought leadership, build credibility, and drive awareness of their product, ultimately leading to increased user adoption and growth.

How I use OPAs

In the last section, let me share my internal process of leveraging OPAs.

I have broken it down into steps so you can replicate it for your business:

Other People's Podcasts

Reach out to podcast hosts in your industry or niche and offer to be a guest on their shows. Share your expertise, insights, and experiences related to your startup or area of focus.

Use the podcast platform to showcase your knowledge, build credibility, and drive awareness of your startup to the podcast's audience.

Engage with the podcast host and audience by sharing valuable information, answering questions, and providing relevant resources or offers.

Leverage the podcast episode by promoting it on your website, social media channels, and email newsletters to amplify its reach and attract new users to your startup.

Other People's Blogs

Identify popular blogs within your industry or target audience and offer to contribute guest articles or collaborate on co-authored content.

Provide valuable and informative content that aligns with the blog's audience and offers insights or solutions related to your startup's area of expertise.

Use guest blogging as an opportunity to showcase your knowledge, establish yourself as an industry authority, and drive traffic back to your own website or landing pages.

Engage with readers by responding to comments, answering questions, and sharing additional resources or offers related to your startup.

Other People's Email Lists

Collaborate with established influencers, thought leaders, or complementary businesses in your industry to leverage their email lists.

Offer to provide valuable content or exclusive offers to be shared with their email subscribers, providing value to their audience while promoting your startup.

Create compelling lead magnets or opt-in offers that align with the interests and needs of the email list's subscribers to encourage sign-ups and drive traffic to your own email list or landing pages.

Ensure that your content or offers resonate with the email list's audience and provide a clear call-to-action to encourage engagement and conversions.

Other People's Events

Identify relevant industry conferences, trade shows, or events where your target audience is likely to be present.

Seek opportunities to speak at these events or participate in panel discussions, sharing your insights and expertise.

Utilize the event platform to showcase your startup's products, services, or solutions through demos, presentations, or interactive experiences.

Network with attendees, industry influencers, and potential customers to build relationships, generate leads, and drive awareness of your startup.

Other People's Webinars

Collaborate with experts, influencers, or complementary businesses to co-host webinars that provide value to your target audience.

Share your knowledge, insights, or case studies related to your startup's industry or niche during the webinar.

Promote the webinar through your own marketing channels and encourage attendees to engage with your startup by offering exclusive offers, free trials, or valuable resources.

Leverage the webinar recording by making it available on your website or through gated access, allowing you to continue generating leads and driving engagement even after the live event.

Other People's Communities

Engage with online communities, forums, or social media groups where your target audience actively participates.

Share valuable insights, answer questions, and provide helpful resources related to your startup's area of expertise.

Build relationships with community members by actively participating in discussions, offering support, and demonstrating your expertise.

Avoid overly promotional or spammy behaviour and focus on providing value to the community. This will help establish your startup's reputation and attract potential customers.

Other People's LinkedIn Posts

Engage with LinkedIn posts from industry influencers, thought leaders, or complementary businesses by leaving thoughtful comments, asking questions, or sharing valuable insights.

Offer genuine support and contribute to the conversation, showcasing your expertise and establishing your startup's presence in the industry.

Leverage LinkedIn's networking capabilities to connect with relevant professionals, potential customers, or industry partners.

Share valuable content from your own startup's LinkedIn page, such as blog articles, infographics, or success stories, to attract engagement and drive traffic to your website or landing pages.

Remember, when leveraging other people's platforms or channels, it is important to provide value, be authentic, and build genuine relationships. By focusing on delivering quality content, engaging with the audience, and aligning with the interests of the channel's users, you can effectively leverage OPAs to expand your startup's reach and drive growth.

Chapter 30

Finding Your Winner Growth Stack

As you run growth experiments, you will be building your growth stack.

A growth stack is the stack of the workflows, tools, and channels that you have experimented with in the past.

Every marketer should have their growth stack documented.

Each business and startup should also maintain its growth stack.

The way I approach this is I maintain a stack for each business that I work with.

I prefer using Google Sheets while you can use any method for building your growth stack.

Let us start with the components of the growth stack.

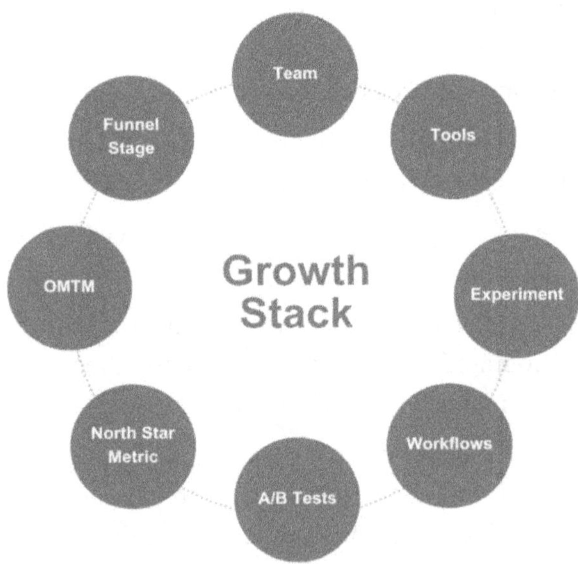

Components of your Growth Stack

- Experiments
- Workflows executed

- A/B Tests conducted
- North Star
- OMTM
- Funnel Stage
- Team
- Tools

Now, let us explore each of the above components in detail, so you can see how to document them and how the same can help you in future.

Experiments (Both successful and unsuccessful)

In your growth stack, you should maintain a record of all the experiments you have conducted, including both successful and unsuccessful ones.

For each experiment, document the objective, hypothesis, and the specific tactics or strategies implemented.

By keeping track of your experiments, you can refer back to them for insights, learnings, and potential future iterations.

Workflows Executed (Variants of workflows under each experiment should be documented)

Under each experiment, document the workflows executed. This includes the step-by-step processes, tasks, and actions taken to implement the experiment.

It is important to document not only the primary workflow but also any variants or iterations that were tested.

This allows you to assess the effectiveness of different approaches and understand which workflows yield the best results.

A/B Tests Conducted (Split testing done for each workflow)

When running experiments, it is crucial to conduct A/B tests to compare and analyse different versions or variations of your workflows.

Document the details of each A/B test conducted, including the specific elements being tested, the control group, and the test group.

Capture the data and results of these tests, including the statistical significance and the impact on the desired metrics. This information will help you make data-driven decisions and iterate on your workflows.

North Star (Main goal of the business for which the experiment was conducted)

For each experiment, clearly define the North Star metric, which represents the primary goal or objective of the business.

This metric should align with the overarching growth objectives and key results the organization aims to achieve.

By documenting the North Star metric for each experiment, you can assess the impact and contribution of the experiment towards the overall growth of the business.

OMTM (The key metric of that particular experiment)

Alongside the North Star metric, identify the specific key metric that is being targeted for improvement in each experiment.

This is referred to as the "One Metric That Matters" (OMTM) for that particular experiment. It could be a conversion rate, user engagement metric, revenue metric, or any other relevant metric that directly reflects the success of the experiment.

Track and analyse the OMTM to evaluate the effectiveness of your experiments and determine their impact on the desired outcomes.

Funnel Stage (The stage of the funnel for which the experiment was conducted from the A3R3 funnel)

Associate each experiment with the specific stage of the A3R3 funnel for which it was conducted.

The A3R3 funnel represents the stages of Awareness, Acquisition, Activation, Revenue, Retention, and Referral.

By mapping each experiment to its corresponding stage, you can better understand which areas of the funnel require improvement and which strategies are most effective at each stage.

Team (Team members and other growth marketers involved in the experiment)

Document the team members and growth marketers involved in each experiment. This includes the individuals responsible for ideation, execution, data analysis, and reporting.

By keeping track of team involvement, you can identify the key contributors to successful experiments and facilitate collaboration and knowledge sharing within your team.

Tools (which tools were used to execute the workflows under the experiment):

Record the tools and technologies utilized to execute the workflows under each experiment.

This includes the analytics platforms, marketing automation tools, A/B testing tools, CRM systems, and any other tools relevant to the experiment.

By documenting the tools used, you can identify which tools are most effective for specific types of experiments and workflows, and make informed decisions when selecting and optimizing your growth stack.

I document all this on a Google Sheet, and I create one sheet per client or business that I work with.

I also add the SPICE score for each experiment to the sheet in order for me to be able to filter out or sort the sheet by the highest score to the lowest score experiments.

Calculating the SPICE Score

The SPICE score is a framework that evaluates experiments based on five key dimensions: Scalability, Past Data, Impact, Confidence, and Ease. Reviewing the SPICE score provides a comprehensive understanding of the experiment's effectiveness and allows you to make data-driven decisions moving forward.

The formula for calculating the SPICE score can be represented as:

SPICE = (Scalability * 0.3) + (Past Data * 0.25) + (Impact * 0.3) + (Confidence * 0.1) + (Ease * 0.05)

Let us further explore each dimension of the SPICE score:

Scalability: Assess the scalability of the experiment, which refers to its potential for implementation on a larger scale. Consider the resources required, the feasibility of expanding the experiment to a broader audience or market segment, and the potential impact at scale.

Past Data: Examine the relevance and utilization of past data in the experiment. Evaluate whether the experiment was informed by historical data, customer insights, or market trends. Assess the extent to which past data influenced decision-making and experiment design.

Impact: Evaluate the impact of the experiment on the desired metric or North Star goal. Measure the magnitude of the effect and the overall contribution to business growth. Consider the significance of the results in relation to the experiment's objectives and the potential long-term impact.

Confidence: Assess the level of confidence in the experiment's results. Consider the statistical significance of the findings, the reliability of the data collected, and the rigor of the experiment design. Evaluate the confidence level in the conclusions drawn from the experiment.

Ease: Consider the ease of execution and implementation of the experiment. Evaluate factors such as the resources required, time investment, and complexity of the experiment. Assess how easily the experiment can be replicated or adapted for future use.

By reviewing the SPICE score of growth marketing experiments, you gain a holistic perspective on their effectiveness.

Experiment Name	Workflow	North Star	OMTM	Funnel Stage	Team	Tools	SPICE Score
Product Trials	1. Set up landing page and promote on website and social media 2. Provide access to the product trial 3. Follow up with users and encourage them to upgrade	Increase number of product trial signups by 20% in 6 months	Get 10 new users to sign up for the product trial in 30 days	Activation	Haris	Unbounce, HubSpot	92
Website A/B Testing	1. Identify page with low conversion rate 2. Create variation of the page with changes 3. Test and compare the two versions	Increase website conversion rate by 10% in 6 months	Improve conversion rate of the identified page by 3% in 30 days	Conversion	Swati	Google Optimize, Google Analytics	90
Lead Magnet	1. Create an irresistible lead magnet 2. Promote lead magnet on website and social media 3. Collect leads	1000 new email subscribers in 6 months	100 new email subscribers in 30 days	Awareness	Haris	Mailchimp, Canva	88

I use the SPICE score column to prioritize future experiments based on their SPICE score, focusing on those with the highest potential for delivering meaningful results.

Growth Stack Example

Next Let us look at an example of a growth stack.

This is just for reference to show you the various columns that would be needed to be documented:

Experiment	Workflows Executed	A/B Tests Conducted	North Star	OMTM	Funnel Stage	Team	Tools
Social Media Campaign	3 variants of ad creatives targeting different demographics	A/B test on ad copy and CTA button color	Double sign-ups on landing page	Conversion rate from ad to sign-up	Acquisition	Growth Marketer, Graphic Designer	Facebook Ads Manager, Google Analytics, Mailchimp
Email Drip Campaign	2 variants of email sequences based on user segmentation	A/B test on subject lines and call-to-action buttons	Improve engagement rate of subscribers by 50%	Click-through rate of emails	Activation	Growth Marketer, Email Copywriter	Mailchimp, Google Analytics
Referral Program	Design and implementation of a referral program with incentives	A/B test on referral bonus structure	Increase referral sign-ups by 30%	Number of referrals per user	Referral	Growth Marketer, Developer	Referral Hero, Google Analytics

You can be more specific in your growth stacks like I do, mentioning names of people you have worked with, specific features of tools you used, and so forth.

How to Leverage the Growth Stack for Future Experimentation

The growth stack plays a vital role in the future of a growth marketer by providing a valuable reference and resource.

Here is how the growth stack can be useful:

Knowledge and Insights

The growth stack serves as a repository of past experiments, workflows, and A/B tests conducted. It allows growth marketers to revisit their previous strategies, learnings, and insights.

By analysing the documented information, growth marketers can gain valuable knowledge about what worked and what did not in the past. This knowledge can inform future decision-making, helping to refine strategies and avoid repeating unsuccessful experiments.

Benchmarking and Comparison

The growth stack enables growth marketers to benchmark and compare the performance of different experiments. By reviewing the documented results, metrics, and outcomes, growth marketers can identify patterns and trends.

They can assess the effectiveness of various workflows, allowing them to identify the most successful approaches. This benchmarking process helps in setting realistic expectations and establishing performance benchmarks for future experiments.

Iterative Improvement

The growth stack facilitates an iterative approach to growth marketing. It allows growth marketers to iterate and build upon previous experiments and workflows. By referring to the growth stack, growth marketers can identify areas for improvement and implement iterative changes in their strategies.

Collaboration and Knowledge Sharing

The growth stack serves as a collaborative tool for the growth marketing team. It allows team members to access and review past experiments, workflows, and results. This fosters knowledge sharing, as team members can learn from each other's experiences and build upon each other's insights.

The growth stack facilitates effective communication, enabling team members to discuss and brainstorm ideas based on the documented information. This collaborative approach enhances the overall effectiveness of the growth marketing efforts.

I also personally use this to re-hire team members or freelancers I worked with in the past, if I get similar projects from startups or businesses in the future.

Since I know they have successfully executed the campaigns for a similar business or campaign in the past, I can be more confident of hiring them again.

Scalability and Efficiency

As the growth stack grows over time, it becomes a valuable resource for scalability and efficiency.

You can reuse effective workflows, adapt A/B test variants, and employ similar tools to streamline the execution of growth experiments. This scalability and efficiency enable growth marketers to optimize their time and resources, leading to improved productivity and accelerated growth.

The growth stack provides a knowledge base, enables benchmarking and comparison, facilitates iterative improvement, supports collaboration and knowledge sharing, and enhances scalability and efficiency.

By leveraging the insights and information within the growth stack, growth marketers can make informed decisions, refine their strategies, and drive sustainable growth for their businesses.

Chapter 31

Measuring Your Own Success

As growth marketers, it is easy to think of our client or startup's success if our success.

But I feel we should have our own North Star, and continuously work toward improving that.

Sometimes, we will be able to find winners in experiments. In other cases, we may not be able to find something despite a lot of experimentation.

There are often factors outside our control when it comes to driving growth.

This is why growth is such an important role.

It is in fact the only thing startups are about.

Remember, Startups = Growth

But it is important to note that one successful growth campaign does not make you a successful growth marketer.

For me, personally, it is about being able to repeat success multiple times.

And not just that, it is more important that more of those experiments become successful as you improve your own skills and intuition over time, as well as collect more data.

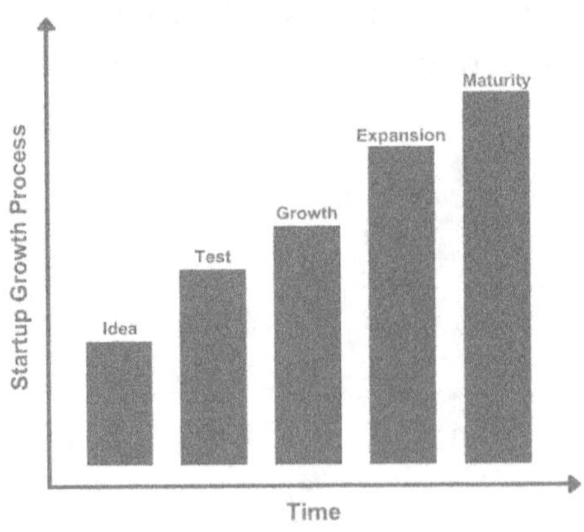

Why failure is not useful as you Grow

This is a hot take as the startup ecosystem glamorizes failure:

Failure is good for you.

As a growth marketer, no one wants to hire you if you are executing to failure.

Over time, you should be able to show startups more success as a growth marketer.

You want more successful experiments that what we did before.

There is no way to eliminate failed experiments, but the ratio of successful experiments should improve over time on your growth marketing journey.

This is how you can charge more from your future clients or in your next job because you can pretty much guarantee that with a few experiments, you can eventually find winners and successful experiments.

That is what startups will pay you for - not for your failures.

This is why I define my own north star metric as something I call the ESR which stands for Experiment Success Rate.

Your Own North Star Metric: Experiment Success Rate

ESR (Experiment Success Rate) is a powerful metric that tracks the percentage of growth experiments that have been successful over a specific period of time.

It serves as a key indicator of a growth marketer's ability to generate impactful insights, drive meaningful outcomes, and deliver value to the business.

Here is how ESR can be beneficial in measuring experiment success:

- **Quantifying Success:** ESR provides a quantitative measure of success by determining the percentage of experiments that have yielded positive results.

- Focus on Continuous Improvement: ESR encourages growth marketers to constantly improve their experimentation methodologies and techniques.

- **Identifying Winning Strategies:** Through ESR analysis, growth marketers can identify the strategies and tactics that consistently lead to successful outcomes.

- **Resource Allocation:** ESR assists in allocating resources efficiently by highlighting the experiments that deliver the most significant impact.

- **Proof of Expertise:** A high ESR serves as a powerful validation of a growth marketer's expertise and competency. It demonstrates their ability to generate insights, make data-driven decisions, and execute strategies that yield positive results.

- **Learning and Adaptation:** ESR enables growth marketers to learn from both successful and failed experiments. By analysing the factors contributing to success, marketers can refine their strategies and replicate effective approaches.

- **Benchmarking and Goal Setting:** ESR can be used as a benchmark to compare performance against industry standards or competitors.

Before we can calculate ESR, we need to maintain a database of growth experiments we did.

Your database of Growth Experiments

Maintaining a database of past growth experiments is crucial for growth marketers as it provides a valuable resource for future decision-making and optimization. Here is how to establish and maintain a database of growth experiments, and the benefits it can offer:

Centralized Experiment Database

Create a centralized database or system to store all relevant information about your growth experiments. This can be a spreadsheet, project management tool, or a dedicated experiment tracking software.

Ensure it is easily accessible and well-organized.

I personally use Google Sheets but you can use the platform you are most comfortable with.

Stick to something you actually use, even if it is not specialized for the purpose.

Capture Experiment Details

Record essential details for each experiment, such as experiment title, objectives, hypothesis, variables tested, metrics tracked, duration, and the overall outcome. Include any additional information that may be relevant, such as target audience, campaign materials, and insights gained.

Track Metrics and Results

Document the key metrics tracked during the experiment and record the results obtained. Include both quantitative and qualitative data to gain a comprehensive understanding of the experiment's impact. This may involve tracking conversion rates, engagement metrics, revenue generated, user feedback, or any other relevant metrics.

Analyse and Document Insights

Once an experiment is completed, take the time to analyse the results and extract valuable insights. Document the key findings, trends, patterns, and lessons learned from each experiment. This includes identifying successful strategies, optimization opportunities, and areas for improvement.

Categorize and Tag Experiments

Categorize your experiments based on different dimensions, such as campaign type, target audience, channel, or objective. Assign relevant tags to experiments to enable easy search and retrieval of specific experiments based on specific criteria. This allows you to filter and analyse experiments based on specific attributes or patterns.

Continuously Update the Database

Regularly update the database with new experiments and their corresponding outcomes. Capture any revisions, iterations, or adjustments made to previous experiments. This ensures that your database remains comprehensive and up-to-date, serving as a reliable source of historical information.

Utilize Insights for Future Experiments

The database of past growth experiments becomes a valuable resource for future decision-making. Analyse the trends, patterns, and insights gathered from previous experiments to inform and optimize future experiment design. Leverage successful strategies, avoid repeating unsuccessful approaches, and build upon past learnings to drive continuous improvement.

Benefits of Maintaining a Database of Growth Experiments

- **Knowledge Preservation:** The database serves as a repository of institutional knowledge, ensuring that insights and learnings are not lost over time or due to team transitions.

- **Data-Driven Decision Making:** By referencing past experiments, you can make informed decisions backed by data and insights, reducing guesswork, and increasing the chances of success.

- **Iterative Optimization:** Reviewing past experiments helps identify optimization opportunities and refine strategies for future experiments, enabling continuous improvement and growth.

- **Benchmarking and Performance Tracking:** Track the progress of specific metrics and experiment success rates over time, allowing you to benchmark and assess the effectiveness of your growth efforts.

- **Efficient Experimental Design:** The database can serve as a reference point for designing new experiments, leveraging successful past approaches, and avoiding previous pitfalls.

By maintaining a database of past growth experiments, you can leverage the collective knowledge and insights gained over time to inform your future experimentation efforts, drive continuous growth, and make data-driven decisions.

Calculating ESR

Calculating the Experiment Success Rate (ESR) involves tracking and evaluating the outcomes of your growth experiments.

Success, in this context, is defined as achieving the goal set for each experiment, typically aligned with the key metric of the month (OMTM).

Here is how you can calculate ESR and track your growth experiments effectively:

Set Clear Experiment Goals

Before launching any experiment, define specific and measurable goals that align with the OMTM. This could be increasing user engagement, improving conversion rates, boosting revenue, or any other relevant metric for your business.

Designate Success Criteria

Determine the specific threshold or target that signifies success for each experiment. This could be a percentage increase in the desired metric, reaching a specific number of conversions, or surpassing a predefined benchmark. Clearly define what constitutes a successful outcome for each experiment.

Track Experiment Outcomes

As you execute your growth experiments, diligently track, and measure the results. Monitor the impact on the targeted metric and compare it against the success criteria set for each experiment. Keep detailed records of the experiment setup, variables tested, and the observed outcomes.

Calculate Success Rate

To calculate the ESR, divide the number of successful experiments by the total number of experiments conducted over a given period.

For example, if you conducted 10 experiments and achieved the desired outcomes in 8 of them, your ESR would be 8/10 or 80%.

I usually like to keep the period as 12 months.

For the first few years of my career, I did not track my ESR.

I started tracking in 2016 and I have been tracking my ESR over the past 6+ years in 12-month periods.

Factors

Analyse the factors that contributed to the success of each experiment. Identify common patterns, strategies, or tactics that led to positive outcomes.

This analysis will help you refine your future experiments and identify areas where you can consistently generate success.

Learn from Failures

It is essential to learn from experiments that did not meet the success criteria. Analyse the reasons behind the failures, identify potential gaps or issues in your approach, and use these insights to improve future experiments.

Learning from failures is as important as celebrating successes to continuously enhance your growth strategies.

Iterate and Optimize

Use the insights gained from successful experiments to refine and optimize your growth strategies. Apply the strategies that have consistently yielded positive results and experiment with variations to drive further improvements. Continuously iterate and refine your approach based on the outcomes and learnings from each experiment.

Track ESR Over Time

Regularly track and analyse your ESR over time. Aim to increase the success rate by refining your experiment design, implementing data-driven strategies, and applying insights from previous experiments.

A rising ESR indicates continuous growth and improvement in your experimentation efforts.

And this is your north star metric.

The metric that will help you become a better growth marketer over time.

I wish you all the best for your growth marketing journey, and an ever-growing ESR over time.

Hope you achieve your north star metric for both yourself and the startups you work with.

Best wishes,

Rish Dev

Special Message from the Author

As we conclude this journey, remember that learning and growth are lifelong pursuits.

The pages of this book are just the beginning of your quest for knowledge and success.

If you have found value in these words, I would like to invite you to join me on this journey to growth.

I have launched GrowthGrad, a community for people like you and me to achieve growth together.

We are a group who is creating success stories together and sharing the journey along the way.

In our community, you will not only deepen your understanding of growth marketing, but also have the opportunity to connect with like-minded individuals who share your passion for continuous learning and achievement.

Together, we can elevate our skills and aspirations to new heights.

Visit us at growthgrad.in to learn more about the community and join us.

See you there.

All the best on your journey to growth.

Rishabh Dev